'This book stands high in my list of best social author's own life and work in Northern Ireland, authenticity. The frequent examples ground Hee..., tail, revealing the messy reality of practice through a series of conversations. The book is a powerful exposition of the complex dynamic of the personal, the professional and the political in the context of communal and common violence. I strongly recommend it.'

Mark Doel, Emeritus Professor, Sheffield Hallam University

'When reading this book you will feel like you are having a conversation with Gerry Heery and you will learn so much from his compassion, humility, and wisdom derived from many years of working with people who have been violent.'

Tim Chapman, Visiting Lecturer, Ulster University

'Social workers and other helping professionals often work with both the victims and perpetrators of violence – often at the same time. In this illuminating book Gerry Heery has brought his wealth of practice experience to doing what many other books fail to do – setting out how to engage and work with those who are violent towards others in their everyday relationships. Underpinned by sound academic scholarship, this is a well-written and helpful resource, and both new and experienced practitioners will find it an invaluable aid.'

John Devaney, PhD, Centenary Professor of Social Work, University of Edinburgh

Promoting Non-Violence

The use of violence within relationships, families or communities is a major public health issue across the world. As such, it will continue to require global, strategic and preventative measures across educational, social care and criminal justice systems. This book draws upon the author's gritty practice experience, social work values, knowledge and research to provide detailed guidance on how to best respond directly to those who carry out this common violence.

Eight face-to-face conversations between a social worker and the person using violence are depicted and used to present the necessary elements for a dialogue which continually seeks to promote non-violence. These conversations pick up on some key messages from the successful Northern Ireland Peace Process and are firmly rooted in social work practice. They will also contribute to the difficult risk decisions that always need to be taken when violence is being used. The reader is offered choice and discretion as to how these conversations can be used by social workers, from short opportunity-led interactions to lengthier, more structured interventions – promoting non-violence.

Offering a positive response to the challenge of 'common' violence in a clear and accessible manner, this book should be considered essential reading for students, researchers and practitioners. The author's royalties will be donated to a third world charity project working with victims of domestic violence.

Gerry Heery is a registered Independent Social Worker, Trainer and Consultant. He began his career as a residential social worker in 1978 and has continued to work with people across the family and childcare and criminal justice systems in Belfast and Northern Ireland. Much of his practice has been with those whose use of violence is causing harm and distress within relationships, families and communities. He has contributed to, developed and published a range of interventions aimed at helping those who have been using such violence to desist.

He lives in Belfast with his wife Máire, and has five children and two grandchildren.

Promoting Non-Violence

Social Work Conversations about Violence

Gerry Heery

Routledge
Taylor & Francis Group
LONDON AND NEW YORK

First published 2019
by Routledge
2 Park Square, Milton Park, Abingdon, Oxon OX14 4RN

and by Routledge
711 Third Avenue, New York, NY 10017

Routledge is an imprint of the Taylor & Francis Group, an informa business

© 2019 Gerry Heery

The right of Gerry Heery to be identified as author of this work has been asserted by him in accordance with sections 77 and 78 of the Copyright, Designs and Patents Act 1988.

All rights reserved. No part of this book may be reprinted or reproduced or utilised in any form or by any electronic, mechanical, or other means, now known or hereafter invented, including photocopying and recording, or in any information storage or retrieval system, without permission in writing from the publishers.

Trademark notice: Product or corporate names may be trademarks or registered trademarks, and are used only for identification and explanation without intent to infringe.

British Library Cataloguing-in-Publication Data
A catalogue record for this book is available from the British Library

Library of Congress Cataloging-in-Publication Data
Names: Heery, Gerry, author.
Title: Promoting non-violence: social work conversations about violence / Gerry Heery.
Description: Abingdon, Oxon; New York, NY: Routledge, 2019. | Includes bibliographical references and index.
Identifiers: LCCN 2018026706 | ISBN 9781138097551 (hardback) | ISBN 9781138097575 (pbk.) | ISBN 9781315104829 (ebook)
Subjects: LCSH: Social service—Practice. | Nonviolence. | Violence—Prevention.
Classification: LCC HV10.5 .H393 2019 | DDC 363.32—dc23LC record available at https://lccn.loc.gov/2018026706

ISBN: 978-1-138-09755-1 (hbk)
ISBN: 978-1-138-09757-5 (pbk)
ISBN: 978-1-315-10482-9 (ebk)

Typeset in Bembo
by codeMantra

Printed in the United Kingdom
by Henry Ling Limited

For Dáire and Ronan

Contents

Acknowledgements	xi
Introduction	1

PART I
Engaging with common violence — 9

1	Personal encounters with violence	11
2	Understanding violence	21
3	Social work and violence	33
4	Risk and violence	44

PART II
Promoting non-violence : the eight conversations and the wall — 55

5	Dialogue and the conversations	57
6	Conversation 1: The 'why' question	62
7	Conversation 2: What is there to talk about?	72
8	Conversation 3: My story and violence	79
9	Conversation 4: The harm I have caused	88
10	Conversation 5: Punching holes in my thinking towards non-violence	94

11 Conversation 6: Dealing with feeling and non-violence	103
12 Conversation 7: Conflict, power and non-violence	111
13 Conversation 8: Keep on keeping on towards non-violence	119
Conclusion	126

Appendices
1 Resource sheets	129
2 Guidance on engaging with victims/survivors	164
Index	167

Acknowledgements

Engaging with people who were using violence within some aspect of their life has been a feature of my social work career from my early experiences as a student on placement in the mid-1970s. Since then I have worked across a range of situations in which I have been able to keep developing my practice within this area. There have been difficult times, but through it all I have been supported and inspired by many colleagues, too numerous to mention. These have been fellow practitioners, as well as those in educational, management and governance settings. This has continued throughout my career. I want to acknowledge this empowering, creative and dynamic Northern Irish Social Work context within which I have been privileged to work. It has contributed greatly to the ideas presented in this publication.

A much smaller group of people have had more involvement in the production of this book:

Kathleen Creaney, a Belfast-based social worker, read and provided feedback on much of the manuscript with wonderful insights and comments.

Mark Doel, with whom I was involved in relation to other matters, took the photograph of the Belfast 'peace wall' (see p. 5) during one of his visits to Belfast.

Several other people kindly read the draft introduction and encouraged me to persevere. These were Christine Smith, Social Work lead within the Department of Health in Northern Ireland, Catherine Maguire, Paul Rooney, Marian O'Rourke and Sharon Mc Ateer (Northern Ireland Social Care Council), Judith Mullinieux, and Mary Mc Colgan from Ulster University, and Carole Kirk (Northern Health and Social Care Trust).

Finally, to my wife Máire. In 2000 she supported me through the trials and tribulations of my first book. At that time, I promised her faithfully that it would be the last. Three books later she has once again been the 'jargon buster' that is vital to my writing. I can never express my love and appreciation to her other than promising that this will be my last book!

Of course, any shortcomings in the book are mine.

Introduction

The photograph

I have one precious photograph taken of myself and three young men, each of whom I worked with for a period of approximately ten years. I first knew them in a residential setting in Belfast where they spent time as teenagers. My relationships continued with them and their families into their adult years as a probation officer working within a community blighted by both social deprivation and the communal and political violence that marred Northern Ireland throughout their lives. There were many elements to my practice. Among others I remember dealing with poverty, educational needs, unemployment, housing issues, parenting, child protection, offending, addiction and mental health difficulties.

Violence, which was both separate from and related to some of the issues referred to, also played a significant role in the lives of each of the young men. They experienced, witnessed and used violence within their families, relationships and community as children and adults. It is their use of violence that is the key area I want to focus on in this book. It was a regular theme in my work as I struggled to help and encourage each of them to move away from the violence that at times dominated and disfigured their lives and relationships. The photograph shows the four of us smiling during a Northern Ireland Probation Service community sports and activity 'day away'. Within ten years of the photo being taken each of the young men was dead. In different ways, violence was associated with the premature and tragic ending of their lives.

A social work career and violence

The stories of the three men were extreme and tragic examples of violence that I have encountered in my social work career. While not always as dramatic, violence, in various forms and to varying degrees, has been a recurring theme across a wide range of social work settings in which

I have worked. I have experienced it with children and young people, older individuals, families, people with mental health difficulties, intellectual difficulties, those with health care issues, and within all communities. Although struggling at times with how best to respond, I have always been curious and indeed fascinated by its occurrence. I have tried to address the violence in each setting in some way. These responses have ranged from those that are brief, ad-hoc and unstructured right across the continuum, to more formal, planned, individualised, group or wider community-based interventions. These have included programmes for men using violent and controlling behaviour within their intimate relationships, parents using aggressive acts towards their children, and young people in trying to help them choose non-violent, safer ways to deal with various situations within their lives (Heery 2001, 2006, 2012).

In summary, I have had thousands of hours of involvement in many practice situations concerned with the use of violence. I have continually thought about and made purposeful efforts to find ways to address the violence. I have reflected on and sought to connect my responses with the theorists, academics and researchers who throughout this period have continued to focus attention on various aspects of violence, particularly within intra-familial situations (Taylor 2013). I have also learned from other practitioners within the learning organisations where I have been privileged to work. In particular, I have gained greater understanding by listening to and talking with those who have been on the receiving end of violence, as well as with those who have used violence. This has contributed to my knowledge base and ability to theorise on the subject of violence. Some of this work has been validated at Advanced, and Leadership and Strategic levels, respectively, within the United Kingdom and Northern Ireland Post Qualifying Social Work frameworks.

This book represents the outcome of my efforts over a period of three years to take stock and pull together this 'practice wisdom', and to give some shape to it. It is offered as a resource to social workers to use in those situations where they are working with someone whose use of violence is causing difficulty. I do this with some trepidation, never forgetting that violence is an enormously complex, multi-determined range of behaviours (Gilligan 2001).

A focus on 'common violence'

Humility in the face of the complexity and vastness of violence within our world is my starting point. I do not and never will have a complete understanding of violence in all its aspects. I am still learning. Social work cannot provide utopian answers to complex human problems and this is particularly so with violence. Furthermore, my focus will be limited. I will not be dealing directly with major violence-filled events such as wars, terrorism, assassinations and genocides which unfortunately continue to cause destruction throughout the world. Having lived through 30 years of violent conflict in Northern Ireland, I am aware that much violence arises out of political and cultural conflicts and how devastating it can be. It is important to acknowledge that many social workers, both within Northern Ireland and further afield, have had to cope with both living through such events themselves while supporting others through the traumas of violence-related experiences.

The focus here will be on the interpersonal violence that many social workers see in the lives of those with whom they work across a range of settings. Nelson Mandela (2002) described this as 'common' violence. The violent behaviour that can occur within relationships, family or social conflict, often though not always, related to personal and property issues (Willman and Makisaka 2011). It is often perpetrated by those we love and trust, by friends and other people we know; for example, through child maltreatment, youth violence, intimate partner violence, child-to-parent violence, elder abuse and sexual violence. Less frequently, it may also be carried out by strangers in random or motivated acts in pursuit of monetary gain or sexual gratification. It may also be an outpouring of hate towards some people because of how they look, who they love, how they pray and just because of who they are.[1] In its various forms, it is a risk factor for lifelong health and social problems, representing a major public health issue across the world (WHO 2014).

Learning from experience

Vivid and gritty examples of my work with the three young men already referred to in the introduction, as well as other practice-related and personal experiences, will bring to life the challenges in addressing common violence in its various manifestations. I will ensure that I protect the identity of those I refer to by using fictitious names and changing key details. When not using a name, I will use the terms 'young person' and 'person' throughout. I will rely on my memory and recollection of incidents, some of them from the distant past. I am aware of how selective and subjective memory can be, and I accept that given human frailty there may be a self-serving element in my recollections. Nevertheless, I will endeavour to reflect events as I believe they happened. I will relate and integrate experiences with relevant theoretical and research-informed material. This will show a complex, messy process, where I have made mistakes and have critically reflected on and learned from my experiences. In doing this I am trying to model an approach that may be helpful to others.

The victims and survivors of violence

Nelson Mandela (2002) emphasised that we should never forget the pain of those who endure common violence. Any intervention with someone who is perpetrating violence should contain a commitment to consider and, if appropriate, prioritise the needs of the victim(s) and survivor(s). Engagement with victims and survivors should be clearly distinguished from the work with those who have perpetrated the violence. A therapeutic response will often be required for someone traumatised by violence. High-quality care and support services are important for reducing trauma, helping people heal and preventing repeat victimisation and perpetration (WHO 2014). Many social workers offer such valuable services. However, other than highlighting a commitment to its provision, this vital and specialist work will not be the focus of this book.

Various community-based and restorative practices seek to bring together the person who has used violence with those on the receiving end. These practices can make valuable contributions to safety and they may be aligned with, or follow on from, the work described in Part II of this volume. Of course, as indicated in Chapter 4 and Appendix 2, they should follow a full risk assessment, including discussion with multi-agency partners and independent support for the 'victim' to allow for a full and informed decision about whether to engage in such a process (Westmarland et al. 2017). They will not be considered within this publication.

There is also the reality that many of those who use violence have also been victims. It is important to listen to and recognise the traumatic past experiences that a person who perpetrates violence may have had in helping him or her move towards safer and non-violent behaviour. A decision may have to be made as to whether a more specialist response related to their victimhood is required for particular individuals. (This issue will be considered further in the third conversation in Part II.)

A significant number of social workers may also be at the receiving end of violence and/or have to respond more directly to it within their professional roles. (This also applies to many colleagues who work in different disciplines across the worlds of social care, education, health and criminal justice.) Again, these important realities will be acknowledged. However, guidance on how to respond in the moment to violent and aggressive behaviour is not offered in this book. There is a wide body of literature available on this challenging practice issue (see e.g. Taylor 2011; Atkins 2015).

The Northern Ireland Peace Process

The Northern Ireland Troubles cast a shadow over much of my personal and professional life.[2] The above photograph is of one of Belfast's many 'peace' walls. This is a misnomer, as they represent division, conflict and violence. Paradoxically, when this particular wall was being built, the first shoots of the Northern Ireland peace process were also emerging.[3] This was instigated by John Hume,[4] who, despite savage criticism, persisted in his efforts to change the language, ideas and ultimately the behaviour of those using politically motivated violence. His vision helped persuade sworn enemies to come together and to address historical differences and enmities through non-violent means. Along with others, a process was created that eventually led to a more peaceful Northern Ireland. Key messages from this peace process are also relevant in working with those who use common violence. The messages provide the inspiration for this book and are the basis for the eight conversations in Part II. Of course, like the peace process there are no guarantees. I still regularly drive past the above wall. It, along with many other walls, still stands, and is a reminder that the potential (and reality) of civil violence remains. This wall will also provide a metaphor for use in each of the conversations in Part II. Removing the wall that is blocking a person's way to non-violence will not be easy.

The book's outline

Part I, 'Engaging with common violence', seeks to build a foundation for practice. Chapter 1 begins with self-knowledge and the importance of addressing our own personal experiences of violence and its impacts before seeking to engage and help with the violence that other people use. This involves reflecting on the psycho-biographical, relational, organisational, political and cultural contexts of violence.

Chapter 2 outlines and analyses a range of the literature and research on violence itself – how it is defined and measured, how it is explained, and current perspectives on how best to respond.

Chapter 3 introduces the social work values and knowledge that are relevant to working with violence. It connects the social work process with the more specialist knowledge from the previous chapter, in proposing the approach outlined in Part II.

Chapter 4 focuses on ensuring that this approach also takes account of the reality of risk that always accompanies violence.

Part II, 'Promoting non-violence: the eight conversations and the wall', aims to encourage a person who is perpetrating violence to become safer. Each conversation ultimately rests on the belief that in order to help someone with their use of violence it needs to be talked through with them. Each conversation also seeks to reflect a key message or issue from the Northern Ireland peace process and to take this forward within relationship-based social work practice (Mc Colgan and Mc Mullan 2017).

The conversations and the various elements within them are offered on the basis of 'take what helps and leave the rest'. Within certain situations and settings, individual elements within particular conversations may be helpful responses for opportunity-led practice. There is also the option to agree with the person to use the conversations in a more structured and planned way, following the language of the current internationally agreed definition of social work, to work together with a person towards Promoting Non-Violence (PNV).[5] Guidance is presented on this in Chapter 5.

A concluding chapter locates the approach within a wider and vital professional and organisational context.

Conclusion

Social workers will often have to engage with a person who is using violence. This publication is ultimately offered as guidance to help with those difficult conversations. It is grounded in both social work values and practice as well as the evidence-informed literature on violence. It may also be a helpful tool for those involved in the training and development of social workers. In addition, it is offered to colleagues in other helping roles such as youth and community, counselling and education. It is offered respectfully, in acknowledgement of the positive work that many helpers already do in such circumstances. While never losing sight of the complexity of violence, the approach seeks to provide a powerful, positive and confident response to the person who is using violence within one or more areas of their life.

Notes

1 President Obama used these or similar words in a speech made in the Safaricom Indoor Arena, Nairobi, Kenya on 26 July 2015.
2 Following centuries of conflict, the 1921 Anglo–Irish Treaty created two states: Northern Ireland, which remained part of the United Kingdom, and the Irish Free State, which eventually became the Republic of Ireland. Northern Ireland comprises two main communities. The 'Unionist/Loyalist' majority group which values and wishes to maintain political union and loyalty to the United Kingdom. The 'Nationalist/Republican' minority group which looks towards an all-Ireland unified state. From its inception, there was deep division between these two main communities in Northern Ireland, a situation made worse by the restricted civil rights experienced by the minority community. The most recent 'troubles' began in the 1960s, continuing for approximately 30 years and coming to an end with the signing of the Good Friday (Belfast) Agreement in 1998. There continues to be tension between the communities. There is also significant fragmentation in each community, which includes groups on both sides which believe in the use of violence to further political aims. Most but by no means all of the majority grouping is from a Protestant background, while most of the minority grouping comes from a Catholic background. Sectarian attitudes and behaviours have been inflamed by, and have also inflamed, the underlying constitutional and political conflict.
3 At the time of writing there are 97 walls or peace barriers still standing across Belfast. Some of these have been there for longer than the Berlin Wall. An interesting short film on these, *When Will the Walls Come Down*, by New Red TV Company Productions, may be accessed on u-tube.
4 John Hume was a political figure in Northern Ireland who did not believe in the use of physical force to achieve political ends. He was awarded the Nobel Peace Prize for his remarkable contribution to the peace process
5 In 2014, the International Federation of Social Workers and International Association of Schools of Social Work agreed the following definition:

> Social work is a practice-based profession and an academic discipline that promotes social change and development, social cohesion, and the empowerment and liberation of people. Principles of social justice, human rights, collective responsibility and respect for diversities are central to social work. Underpinned by theories of social work, social sciences, humanities and indigenous knowledges, social work engages people and structures to address life challenges and enhance wellbeing.

References

Atkins, B. (2015) *Personal Safety for Social Workers and Health Professionals*. Critical Publishing.
Gilligan, J. (2000) *Violence: Reflections on our Deadliest Epidemic*. London: Jessica Kingsley.
Heery, G. (2001) *Preventing Violence in Relationships*. London: Jessica Kingsley.
Heery, G. (2006) *Parents Anger Management Programme*. Lyme Regis: Russell House Publishing.

Heery, G. (2012) *Equipping Young People to Choose Non-Violence*. London: Jessica Kingsley.
Mandela, N. (2002) in *World Report on Violence and Health*. Geneva: WHO.
Mc Colgan, M. and McMullin, C. (2017) *Doing Relationship Based Social Work: A Practical Guide to Building Relationships and Enabling Change*. London: Jessica Kingsley.
Taylor, B. (2011) *Working with Aggression and Resistance in Social Work*. London: Learning Matters.
Taylor, B. (2013) *Professional Decision Making and Risk in Social Work*. London: Learning Matters.
Westmarland, N., Johnson, K. and Mc Glynn, C. (2017) Under the Radar: The Widespread Use of 'Out of Court Resolutions' in Policing Domestic Violence and Abuse in the United Kingdom. *British Journal of Criminology*. Published by Oxford University Press on behalf of the Centre for Crime and Justice Studies (ISTD).
Willman, A. and Makisaka, M. (2011) *Interpersonal Violence Prevention: A Review of the Evidence and Emerging Lessons*. World Development Report Background Paper. Washington, DC: World Bank. © World Bank. Available at https://openknowledge.worldbank.org/handle/10986/9142. Licence: CC BY 3.0 IGO.
World Health Organisation (2014) *Global Statistics Report on Violence Prevention*. Geneva: WHO.

Part I

Engaging with common violence

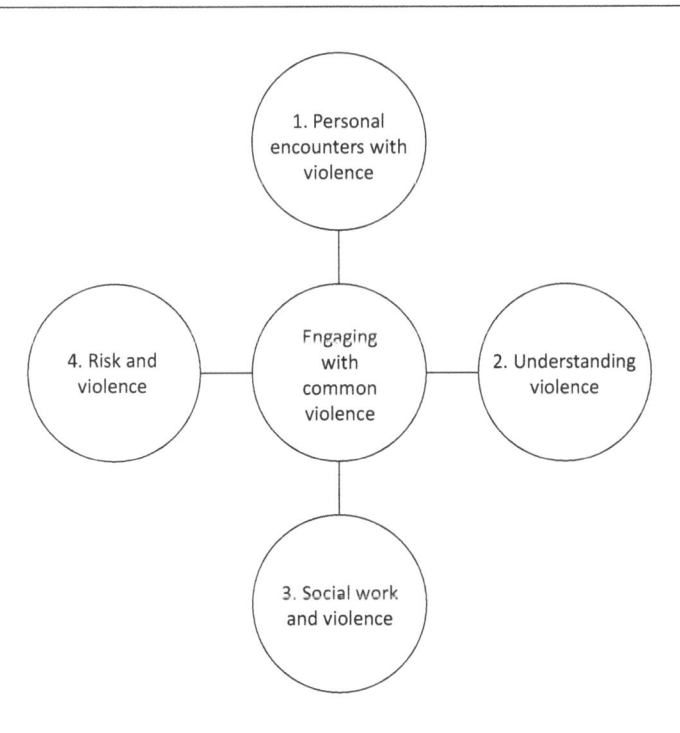

- 1. Personal encounters with violence
- 2. Understanding violence
- 3. Social work and violence
- 4. Risk and violence

Engaging with common violence

Chapter 1

Personal encounters with violence

Introduction

In training, I sometimes ask the group of social workers to take a few moments to reflect silently on any violence inflicted on them within their relationships and family life, their wider community life or their work situations. I ask those who feel that they have never been on the receiving end of violent behaviour to put their hand up. No one to date has raised an arm. A small-scale piece of research took this a little further with a group of social work students who were asked to write about their own experiences as victims of the common violence referred to in the introduction. Their list included 'armed robbery; the unlawful killing of a relative; sexual assault; childhood sexual abuse; neglect; rape and several episodes of domestic violence' (Robbins 2014, p. 5).

This chapter will explore the impact of such encounters with violence. Each person's experience of these will be unique, but needs to be dealt with, both personally and professionally. This is critical if we wish to help someone else address their use of violence. What we do not sort out within ourselves may well be projected onto others (O'Leary 2016). What follows includes an account of my own efforts to do so, as well as associated reflections that may be helpful to others.

Violence within families of origin and relationships

All of us will carry some psychic and emotional wounds arising from experiences within our families, or relationships. To varying degrees, each person will have been on the receiving end of actions that will have caused distress and upset. There is always a need for reconciliation and forgiveness to get back on track and this is what often happens. Family and relationship breakdown can also cause deep and lasting hurt that cannot be minimised.

However, the focus in this section is on those who have gone through serious physical, emotional, sexual or other devastating abuses of power. I was fortunate that in my early family life and relationships, the foundation of trust, love and security remained in place. In many ways, I was naïve about such aspects of life. It was only over time, and through listening to the experiences of those on the receiving end of abuse, that I started to become more aware of and learn about the betrayal and emotional devastation caused by violence within close intimate relationships. My saddest and most traumatic memories from practice are from people whose lives were destroyed by the abuse they suffered.

As the study referred to above suggests, and confirmed by the staggering levels of this violence outlined in Chapter 2, there is every reason to believe that the experience of abuse is a reality in the lives of a significant number of social workers. Is there a danger that, for those who have endured such a legacy, it may 'leak out' and influence how they may engage professionally with those who have perpetrated such behaviours or other forms of violence? I have witnessed harsh judgements, disdain, apprehension and fear from social workers engaging with those who have used violent behaviour. Do such unhelpful reactions sometimes relate to past experience of abuse? Was this possibly the case in relation to the behaviour of the social worker below?

Example 1 'The letter'

Amir left his war-torn country to move to a European city. Some five years later, aged 34, he met and began a relationship with Jane who was studying in the same city. Following the completion of her studies Jane returned to her family home and, despite lengthy separations, their relationship continued, and they had a child who lived with Jane in Northern Ireland. Following an incident shortly after the birth of the child, Amir was convicted of a domestic violence offence against Jane. He spent some time in prison in the European city. The couple subsequently reconciled, and they agreed that Amir should travel to Northern Ireland where they would live together as a family. Social services became aware of his conviction, and he and Jane were informed that he would only be allowed supervised contact with the child until a full assessment of their situation had been completed. This risk assessment will be returned to in Chapter 4.

Amir initially had no official status to live in Northern Ireland, and resided in a small, poorly maintained terraced house with several other men – all seeking asylum. He was barred from working or claiming benefits and had to live on £10 per week, relying on food banks to get enough to eat.

Amir was very anxious to see his child regularly and depended on travel warrants being sent to his address so that he could make the journey. On one occasion, I called to see him at his accommodation. When we found a quiet corner in the damp, poorly furnished house he showed me a torn-open envelope with the address of the house on it. He was upset and his first words to me were: 'She never even put my name on the envelope. Someone else opened this and knows my business now. I'm no better than something she walks on.' He continued in tears: 'I know the way she looks at me, she thinks of me as some sort of monster!' He didn't accept my suggestion that it may have been a mistake. He was adamant that I should not raise the matter. The failure of the social worker to put his name on a letter sent to him spoke powerfully to Amir.

I never spoke with the social worker about this incident and I cannot be sure about the motivation. It may have been an entirely unintentional oversight. Alternatively, it may have reflected racial prejudice towards Amir. I do not know. However, I did sense a strong aversion towards Amir's behaviour and towards him. I wondered if this may have had its roots in the social worker's previous and personal traumatic experiences of control and abuse.

Of course, past abusive experiences will not automatically impact negatively upon practice. I have worked with and been inspired by colleagues who have dealt with such experiences, and indeed used them to work sensitively and compassionately in helping someone appreciate more fully the effects of violence on others. The importance of the contribution of practitioners to the work who are also survivors of domestic violence is now well recognised (Hague and Mullender 2006). They have been able to cope with deep psychological and emotional wounds, and in ways that have made them stronger and special (Biddulph 1997).

Violence within communities and society

Growing up in Belfast and Northern Ireland I encountered violence. As a child from the Nationalist, mainly Catholic community, I quickly became aware that my identity could sometimes put me at risk. I remember being attacked and then having to avoid certain areas on my way to and from school, and a growing sense of difference, hostility and conflict. As a teenager, my family home was attacked, forcing a move to a different part of the city. When I married, our first home was in a 'mixed' area of the city. Following the sectarian murders of several people living in the vicinity and attacks on several houses, including my own, I once again, as my parents had done 15 years previously, moved to a 'safer' area. My home, and those of my neighbours, was demolished. In their place was built the brick wall with the high fence on top (18 metres in height). This is the same wall referred to and shown in the introduction.[1]

Twenty years of my working life were spent within a context of communal, political and sectarian violence, within a mainly nationalist area in Belfast. Years of discrimination and neglect had resulted in it being one of the poorest and most socially deprived areas of the United Kingdom at that time. Social adversities were further compounded by the continuing armed conflict between paramilitary groups seeking a political change and unification of Ireland and the police and military forces of Northern Ireland and the United Kingdom. The main paramilitary group was the Provisional Irish Republican Army (PIRA), whose political representatives were Sinn Féin.[2] My practice often took place within a context of regular outbursts of violence and an unrelenting political struggle for the hearts and minds of an impoverished community. This all-pervasive context of communal violence presented unexpected challenges to my practice.

Example 2 'The choice'

Thomas, one of the young people in the photograph I referred to in the introduction, had been placed on probation following his involvement in car theft and associated offences. He was 21 at the time. As his probation officer I had a good relationship with him, but was making little impact in persuading him to change his behaviour. His offending caused distress to the local community and also saw him clashing with some members of the PIRA who had taken on a quasi-policing role. Their involvement in such a role reflected the general distrust towards and fear of the state police force at the time. I remember Thomas coming to the office and telling me in a rather matter-of-fact way that after ignoring several warnings from the PIRA he was to be 'nutted' (that is, shot in the head). However, he had been given two alternatives, either to leave the country or choose to be shot in both ankles, knees and feet as a 'final chance'. He did not want to leave his home, so his choice was stark – 'one in the head or six'. Although as a probation officer I was not able to engage directly with the PIRA, I had the threat confirmed through a community group who mediated between statutory and illegal organisations. I was shocked when he told me that he had already arranged a time and meeting place for the punishment shooting, and that he would be unable to keep our weekly appointments for a while, as he expected to be in hospital. Sadly, such barbaric 'punishments' carried out by various paramilitary groupings continue to this day.

Many social workers across the world live and work in dangerous wartorn or conflict-ridden areas and in communities beset with inequalities and violence. Like myself, they will probably never fully understand how living through such events has shaped them. They, and I, have had to find our own ways to process and come to terms with these experiences. The main coping tactic for myself and other social workers within the Northern Ireland conflict was probably one of avoidance. We steered away from all aspects of the ongoing 'war', disengaging from analyses of politics, power and conflict, and finding a 'non-political' and 'non-sectarian' approach through the communal conflict. We found that often the safest approach was 'whatever you say, say nothing'![3] Of course, as we see below, this was not always without some difficulty.

Example 3 'Smiling assassins'

On one occasion, I was involved in a meeting between some probation staff and Sinn Féin community representatives. The purpose was to try to find alternatives to the punishment shootings and attacks on young people, like Thomas, who were alleged to be engaging in antisocial behaviour within the community. It was early on in the peace process and a significant number of people viewed Sinn Féin as 'terrorists' because of their close relationship with the PIRA – a view still held by some today. The meeting was cordial and polite. However, the difficulties experienced by some of those at the meeting became clear to me when I suggested shortly after to my manager that the meeting had gone reasonably well. Stern-faced and through gritted teeth, the manager almost spat out how hard it had been to sit across the table from those 'smug smiling assassins'. Many social workers and their agencies have had to, and continue to, work through such feelings of fear, distrust and anger. Violence always leaves a legacy that is rarely fully overcome.

Social workers have consistently promoted positive messages of respect and reconciliation and, in particular, sought to support victims and communities devastated by the troubles. Reflecting the vision of the Chief Probation Officer at that time,[4] the Belfast team in which I worked was proactive in engaging with various voluntary, neighbourhood and victim support bodies. Connections were made to ensure that despite being 'agents of the state' the team was able to operate throughout the most violent of times. One memorable example of innovative practice was the use of sporting activities and the creation of a board game by a colleague to help facilitate safer dialogue between young people from both of the main communities.[5] Hopefully, someday, the full story of all the aspects of positive social work practice throughout the troubles will be told. A forthcoming publication addresses this issue in listening to and exploring some of the stories and challenges from this period (Duffy et al. 2018).

Academic and social work agencies have continued, right up until the present time, to cooperate with victims' groups in working with new generations of social work students. There is a genuine commitment to inform and sensitise the students to the traumatic 'troubles'-related experiences that many of those who use social work services have gone through. It is no coincidence that the current Victims Commissioner is a social worker.[6]

Violence within professional and working lives

Much social work practice is at the interface of pain, poverty and powerlessness (Morrison 2008). Social workers across many settings may occasionally experience this playing out violently against themselves. I first experienced this as a residential social worker, a practice context that can be ambivalent, tempestuous, volatile and sometimes dangerous for children and staff (Howard 2012). I have seen some colleagues deeply impacted by violence and abuse at the hands of already traumatised young people. As indicated in the introduction, comprehensive guidance on how best to deal with these situations will not be provided here. However, as with the other experiences of violence explored in this chapter, they do need to be dealt with. It is critical that organisations support staff through such situations. This does not always happen.

Example 4 On the receiving end of violence

Mary was a committed and experienced practitioner who enjoyed building relationships and supporting young people in residential care. John was a 16-year-old young person who had been in the centre for several months. He had experienced a history of abuse and trauma. He has used violence towards some women in his life. On this occasion, he approached Mary who was standing with some other staff at the front door of the children's home. 'I'm going to cut your throat you fucking whore.' was his opening remark to her; this was followed up with pointing and aggressive gesticulations and continuing verbal abuse as he approached her. Mary held her ground, asking him not to be offensive towards her. John became more threatening and a physical restraint was required by other staff. Mary was upset and distressed by the incident itself, but this was magnified when she was subsequently criticised and disciplined for not quickly withdrawing from the situation. To be fair, the managerial response may have reflected an organisation that was sincerely striving to work therapeutically and wanted to avoid the use of physical restraints and the possibility of re-traumatising a young person. However, not only should Mary have received much more support; the insistence on a 'passive' approach to the young person's aggression was ultimately unsafe for him.

The organisational and professional context of violence is not just about failings in how organisations respond to those situations where violence is emanating from the people receiving services. Organisations themselves, and the way their staff work, may sometimes abuse their power and inflict or compound the violence that those with whom they are working have already experienced. For example, social work's record in supporting the safety and protection of women and children experiencing domestic violence is varied (Laing et al. 2013). I have occasionally experienced situations where the domestic violence experienced by some women has been viewed more as a hurdle the women must overcome rather than as a trauma through which they should be supported (Robbins and Cook 2017).

It can also happen that, as representatives of the state, social work organisations and their staff may sometimes work within harsh laws or other legal, policy or agency contexts, which, for those on the receiving end, can be experienced as oppressive and indeed violent. Example 5 is a personal example of such professional involvement with a young man during the 1980s, James.

Example 5 'A social enquiry report'

James, 22 years old, had pleaded guilty to a charge of homosexual activity with another person aged 19. A report was requested by the court to assist with sentencing. I was part of a system that was seeking to criminalise him because of moral choices he had made in regard to his behaviour. His situation was further complicated and worsened in that he told me that the police said they would drop the charge if he gathered information that might be helpful to them in their efforts to deal with the PIRA (and other paramilitary groupings in the area). Not surprisingly, that caused James further significant emotional and psychological harm. Although he shared it with me, he was adamant that he did not want me to raise it with anyone. It was another case of 'whatever you say, say nothing' He was clear that he wanted to take his chances with the court case – as that, in his view, was the safer of the two options. I remained respectful, compassionate and non-judgemental towards James throughout the process. He received a conditional discharge. I always felt that I had been part of a coercive process.

The law in Northern Ireland has since changed and the offence referred to was removed from the statute book.[7] However, the issue of a coercive legal context can re emerge at any time. For example, at the time of writing, social workers are involved in preparing court reports on people who have been trafficked into the United Kingdom. Some of these people have been kept as modern-day slaves, and then forced into illegal activities such as manufacturing drugs. In effect, social workers are then involved indirectly in the criminalisation of these people and compounding the violence and abuse they have already experienced.[8]

Care also needs to be taken in how work is carried out with those who have been violent. As my practice evolved to working with those who had perpetrated serious sexual abuse against women, children and vulnerable people, I can still recall some early feelings of disgust and disdain that I experienced.

I was reluctant to tell friends and colleagues that I worked directly with people who had sexually abused young children. I initially imagined that in some way I could be 'stigmatised by association' (Travers 1999, p. 120). I struggled to cope with some of my feelings, and became blocked in being open and forthright in dealing with them (Shulman 1999). I was never sure as to how they leaked out in my work with the men who had perpetrated such violence. I may also have revelled in the power that my role gave me in the lives of these men.

Fortunately, as with the personal and communal encounters with violence discussed earlier, I have also witnessed and experienced many positive and creative organisational and professional responses to violence. Many social work agencies do incredible work with those who have suffered abuse and violence. Returning to the issue of supporting women who have experienced domestic violence, I have witnessed much positive practice. Furthermore, many of my experiences have been when tensions have arisen because a woman has wanted to persevere with a relationship with a man who has used violence against her. Social workers have then had to balance this with safeguarding issues not only for the woman herself but also for children who may be involved.

Similarly within residential child care, I have also seen how the use of restorative and various therapeutic approaches has contributed to the safety of staff and young people living together. I have also witnessed colleagues within criminal justice and also child protection engaging sensitively and compassionately with men who have used violence without losing sight of the need to ensure the safety of others.

Such positive practice also reflects a broader context in Northern Ireland where social work agencies and academics have developed strong partnership arrangements in promoting continuous professional development.[9] There is a recognition that the most effective approach in reducing harm and promoting safety is to wholeheartedly embrace an ethic of learning (Berwick 2013). I, and many of my colleagues, have been provided with continuous flexible pathways in which to critically reflect on and develop professional practice and supervision. It has certainly been important for me in seeking to work through some of the issues raised by the encounters with violence shared earlier and in helping to ensure my own well-being. Returning to the example of the limitations in my practice in working with men who had sexually abused children, I was able to resolve these within a team culture of openness, acknowledgement of vulnerability, continuous learning and high levels of support.

Self-awareness

The ability to be self-aware and to regulate emotion is now accepted as a key element within the overall conceptualisation of social work competence (Bogo et al. 2014). In working with those who have used violence, I, and my colleagues, need to ensure that any residual issues, made up of the unhelpful thoughts and feelings from previous experiences, which may be triggered by the person in front of me, are dealt with appropriately (Lehane Sheehan 2012). This will not only lead to more effective and compassionate engagements, but also contribute to resilience in working with violence (Howe 2008). It is only through an ongoing commitment to continual reflecting and learning in relation to practice, as outlined above, that self-awareness and emotional resilience can continue to be nourished (Grant and Kinman 2012). Particularly for experienced social workers, who run the risk of becoming desensitised by violence and seeing it as normal, continued critical reflection, time out and support to recognise its many impacts are essential.

Conclusion

Ultimately, each of us has to gauge for ourselves how well we have processed the various manifestations of the violence which we have experienced throughout our lives. As we have seen, it is a complicated process and the consequences may well be either positive or negative, or both. Nelson Mandela stated starkly, 'As I walked out the door towards the gate that would lead to freedom, I knew if I didn't leave my bitterness and hatred behind, I'd still be in prison' (quoted in Grogan 2015, p. 102). My religious faith, support from my family, community and also from the many resilient colleagues and organisations I have worked with, as well as continued learning, have all played their part in my own journey.

I need to continue to be self-aware about how violence has impacted upon me. It is only in doing so that I will be able to help someone else, who is struggling with their use of violence, to become more aware of its place within their own life. This is the bedrock upon which the conversations outlined in Part II rest, and one of the core messages they offer in promoting non-violence.

Notes

1 There is a statutory scheme in Northern Ireland which purchases the properties of those who have been forced to move from their homes at the current 'market' value of the property. I was much more fortunate than the many millions of refugees who have and continue to flee their homes from various parts of the world, often with nothing more than what they are wearing.
2 The PIRA's political representatives were Sinn Féin who re-emerged as a political force during this period and who were to become part of the power sharing government in Northern Ireland as the peace process gained momentum.
3 Seamus Heaney, Northern Ireland's Nobel Peace Award-winning poet's often quoted remark.
4 Breige Gadd was Chief Probation Officer in Northern Ireland from 1986 to 1998.
5 Maura Muldoon was a colleague on the West Belfast Probation Team.
6 Judith Thompson was a colleague in the Probation Service and we worked together in introducing the early form of a post-qualifying framework into the agency along with other social work agencies and educational establishments.
7 At this time homosexual behaviour between a person over 21 with someone under 21 was a criminal offence in Northern Ireland. This is no longer the case and social workers were among those who advocated for reform.

8 Following lobbying from social workers, among others, Northern Ireland became one of the first jurisdictions in the world to protect victims of trafficking from prosecution for offences they had been forced into – Human Trafficking and Exploitation (Criminal Justice and Support for Victims) Act (Northern Ireland) 2015.
9 This has taken various forms. Currently the NI Social Care Council (NISCC) promotes the Professional in Practice Framework for Continuing Professional Development of qualified social workers.

References

Berwick Report National Advisory Group on the Safety of Patients in England (2013) *A Promise to Learn – A Commitment to Act*. NHS.
Biddulph, S. (1997) *Raising Boys*. London: Thorsons.
Bogo, M., Rawlings, M., Katz, E. and Logie, C. (2014) *Using Simulation in Assessment and Teaching*. Virginia: CSWE Press.
Duffy, J., Campbell, J. and Tosone, C. (eds) (2018) *International Perspectives on Social Work and Political Conflict*. London: Routledge.
Grant, L. and Kinman, G. (2012) Enhancing Wellbeing in Social Work Students: Building Resilience in the Next Generation. *Social Work Education: The International Journal*, 31(5): 605–621.
Grogan, B. (2015) *Making Good Decisions: A Beginners Guide*. Dublin: Veritas.
Hague, G. and Mullender, A. (2006) Who Listens? The Voices of Domestic Violence Survivors in Service Provision in the UK. *Violence against Women*, 8: 687–718.
Howard, N. (2012) The Ryan Report (2009). A Practitioner's Perspective on Implications for Residential Child Care. *Irish Journal of Applied Social Studies*, 12(1), Article 4. Available at https://arrow.dit.ie/ijass/vol12/iss1/4.
Howe, D. (2008) *The Emotionally Intelligent Social Worker*. Basingstoke: Palgrave Macmillan.
Laing, L., Humphreys, C. and Cavanagh, K. (2013) *Social Work and Domestic Violence: Developing Critical and Reflective Practice*. London: Sage.
Lehane Sheehan, M. (2012) *Seeing Anew*. Dublin: Veritas.
Morrison, T. (2008) The Emotional Effects of Child Protection Work on the Worker. *Practice*, 4(4): 253–271. DOI: 10.1080/09503159008416902.
O'Leary, D. (2016) *The Happiness Habit*. Dublin: Columba Press.
Robbins, R. (2014) 'She Knew What was Coming': Knowledge and Domestic Violence in Social Work Education. *Social Work Education*. Available at http://dx.doi.org/10.1080/02615479.2014.898748.
Robbins, R. and Cook, K. (2017) Don't Even Get Us Started on Social Workers: Domestic Violence, Social Work and Trust – An Anecdote from Research. *British Journal of Social Work*. Available at https://doi.org/10.1093/bjsw/bcx125.
Shulman, D. (1999) *The Skills of Helping Individuals, Families, Groups and Communities* (4th edition). Belmont: Wadsworth Thompson Learning.
Travers, O. (1999) *Behind the Silhouettes: Exploring the Myths of Child Sexual Abuse*. Belfast: The Blackstaff Press.

Chapter 2

Understanding violence

Introduction

The previous chapter explored the tendency to see, define and respond to violence in our own way based on individual experience and the context of our lives (Alvarez and Bachman 2013). The purpose of this chapter is to balance and challenge this with reference to literature and research into common interpersonal violence. This is a daunting task, as there has been, and continues to be, a vast amount of study and debate as to the nature of violence. This activity continues across many fields, including sociology, psychology, anthropology, neurobiology, genetics, politics, religion and philosophy. They all contribute in their own ways to the massive jigsaw puzzle of violence.

Attention will be mostly on the human and social sciences. These cannot claim to have exposed the laws and principles that the physical sciences have been able to do (Musson 2017). This is certainly the case with violence. Despite this, but with some trepidation, the chapter will identify and analyse a selection of the evidence-informed literature into violence. It will address four key questions in relation to how it should be defined, measured, explained and, ultimately, responded to. My recollections of the circumstances, as well as some of the behaviour, of another of the young men in the photograph will be used to assist in answering these questions. The example is not put forward as an exact record of what happened but as a way of bringing the questions to life.

Example 6 A day in the life

Simon was staying with his girlfriend Sarah in her flat. He had been drinking significant amounts of alcohol for several days and he was craving another drink. He asked her for a loan and, when she refused, he jumped up in front of her and shouted into her face, 'I just need a fiver for fuck's sake.' When Sarah refused he threatened: 'If you don't lend me something I'll fuckin rip your face of you fat bitch.' Sarah told him to 'fuck off' but, before she could stop him, he took her remaining couple of pounds from her purse. Sarah jumped up and tried to get the money from him, but he shoved her aside. She threw her half-empty cup of tea at him, striking him on the head with it. Lisa, their 2-year-old daughter, then came into the room crying as Simon was leaving. He shouted at Sarah, 'Would you feed that child and clean her up as well as the mess you've made. For fuck's sake, what sort of mother are you?' Sarah, in tears, shouted at the child who was also crying and shoved her back into her bedroom, 'Would you go back to bed and give my head peace. It's your fucking da, he's a bastard!'

Simon needed more money, so he called into his mother's house nearby. He demanded some from her, saying she would get it back when he got his benefits the following day. Seeing his mood, she knew better than to object and gave him £5.

Simon was able to buy some cheap alcohol and spent several hours drinking in a local park with other men. As several schoolgirls walked past them on their way home from school later that day, two of men in the group with Simon started making crude, sexualised comments about them, leaving one of the young girls in tears. Later on that evening, Simon was walking back home when he came upon two other young men with whom he had been involved in a fight a few days previously. He sensed the danger but wasn't quick enough to get away and before he knew it he was being punched and kicked to the ground. Fortunately, some passing women intervened and his two assailants ran off. Bleeding and bruised, Simon struggled back to his mother's house.

Defining violence

The events described in Simon's life in the above example illustrate some of the forms that common violence can take; from one person to another, within intimate relationships, families and communities. During the day, several people behaved in ways that intentionally threatened or actually caused physical, sexual or psychological harm to others (Stanko 2002). The critical features marking the boundary between violence and non-violence are the consequence, control and harm caused by the action (Zink et al. 2004). Actions, intentions and effects all need to be taken into account in defining violence. Simon's actions towards his mother did not appear to be as dramatic or as 'violent' as they were towards Sarah. However, although never subjected to a physical assault, his mother had a sense of dread arising from some of the behaviours which she had been experiencing from Simon for a considerable period. These were having an ongoing mental and psychological impact upon her well-being (Harne and Radford 2008). The reality is that within any relationship, actions that may not in themselves appear to be significant may cumulatively seriously impair a person's psychological integrity. The definition of violence needs to be submerged within such notions of 'abuse' and coercion (Walby et al. 2017).

Violence can also occur even when a 'victim' does not perceive the behaviour as harmful. Following the abusive sexualised comments to the passing schoolgirls, one of the girls became upset and distressed, while another did not and agreed to meet up with one of the young men later. Both were subject to violence. Sexual exploitation, increasingly involving the use of social media, continues to be directed towards young and vulnerable people who are in need of protection. There is now general agreement across the world that such abuse needs to be addressed.[1]

The degree to which some of the other behaviours outlined during Simon's day should be classified as both violent and criminal behaviour is more contentious. The 'point at which someone's aggression towards others (inside or outside of the family) can be considered a violent crime is open to great dispute and historical and cross-cultural variation' (Jones 2008, p. 179). Should Sarah's behaviour towards her child be viewed as a violent crime? Was it reasonable chastisement or unjustifiable assault? I have discussed this with colleagues and we have taken different views. Corporal chastisement of children is accepted in some jurisdictions and not in others. Some aspects of parenting practice in the past are now considered to be child abuse. The formal legal boundary between 'violence' and 'not violence' may be drawn in different places by different people. There will probably always be some uncertainty and the concept of violence will always be contested to a degree and its meaning will remain fluid and not fixed (Stanko 2002).

Measuring violence

None of the occasions of violence during Simon's day ever became an official statistic. Despite many efforts to address this, huge challenges in accurately measuring common violence remain and much of it continues to be unrecorded. A 2014 Europe-wide survey acknowledged that the tensions and differences in the definitions and understanding of violence referred to above also make measurement difficult. In particular, it pointed up the lack of comprehensive data on the scale and nature of the problem of violence against women. It found that much of this violence remained hidden, as victimised women tended not to report the violence to the authorities (FRA 2014).

Moreover, in relation to serious manifestations of violence, such as homicide, the World Health Organisation (2014) estimated that approximately 60 per cent of countries do not have usable data on this. It also stated that less than half of countries reported conducting population-based surveys on other types of violence such as child maltreatment, youth violence and elder abuse.

Allowing for the above limitations, figures that have been produced suggest that there are staggering levels of interpersonal common violence. They indicate that a great deal of such violence is committed by 15- to 30-year-old men – the one great universal in the study of violence (Pinker 2012). One international review concluded that homicide was the third leading cause of death for males aged 15 to 40 across the world (WHO 2014). A more focused Northern Ireland study reported that the presence of conflict and violence in the lives of many young men, like Simon, was not out of the ordinary and that their personal safety was a daily issue (Lloyd 2009).

Women, children and elderly people also bear the brunt of much non-fatal physical, sexual and psychological violence, most of it from men. For example, while writing this book, a survey of women attending a Northern Ireland university revealed alarming levels of exposure to sexual harassment and abuse among female students.[2] Brison's (2002) conclusion that sexual violence was taken for granted because of its prevalence continues to have validity. One in five women report that they had been sexually abused as a child, and one in three a victim of physical or sexual violence at some point in her lifetime (WHO 2014). Much of the violence experienced by women is at the hands of an intimate male partner. Similarly, a review of American research, including data compiled by the US Department of Justice, demonstrated strongly the presence of intra-familial violence in families of every race, religion, social class and educational level, with men again being more likely to be responsible for serious violence (Cismaru and Lavack 2011).

Furthermore, for some women, such violence continues throughout the life course. Neither midlife nor old age protects them from psychological/emotional, control, threat, physical or sexual abuse (Fisher et al. 2010).

Parents, mainly mothers, have also reported increasing levels of violence at the hands of their children, mostly sons. This often brings with it intolerable tension of an overwhelming worry about their child while at the same time a real fear as to what the child may do to them (Jones 2011).

There is also evidence of the use of violence by women, and some would suggest that this has been increasing. An American National Crime Victimisation Survey concluded that almost 20 per cent of robberies (a crime that involves the threat of or actual physical violence) involved female offenders (Alvarez and Bachman 2013). Similarly, there are also studies that now consistently point to men being the victims of violence within their relationships and families at the hands of women (Lovestad and Krantz 2015). Sarah was violent towards Simon and towards her daughter. Indeed, the entire book could be filled with a wide array of research-based accounts of the use of violence by women within many different contexts, including same-sex relationships (See e.g. Kamimura et al. 2017; Buzi et al. 2017).

The identification of the issue of female violence perhaps reflects the scholarship and research evidence that has become more nuanced and has thrown light on the diversity of people both perpetrating and being affected by violence. It is also part of an ongoing and, at times, controversial 'gender symmetry' debate in terms of the use of violence by men and by women. On 16 March 2015, the *British Journal of Criminology* published a special online issue entitled 'Shedding Light on Domestic Violence Research'. It presented a selection of the research from the previous 50 years. Among other issues it addressed the possibility that women were as violent as men. While some of the research appeared to be pointing in this direction there was also a recognition that the majority of those actually working in the service delivery arena, 'at the coal face' – that is, social workers, probation officers, police and accident and emergency staff – took the view that it was generally women who tended to suffer the brunt of most violence and abuse in private life, particularly in terms of injuries and traumatic impact. This would concur with my own experience from 40 years of practice in Northern Ireland.

Given the difficulties in measuring violence referred to above, uncertainty remains as to whether our world is presently more or less violent than in the past. When I began my career in social work in the 1970s many aspects of common violence, particularly within relationships and families, were hidden. Pioneering research, much of it by women (e.g. Evason 1982; McWilliams and McKiernan 1993, among others), helped bring intimate partner violence out into the open. However, has this greater awareness inured us to its continued growth? Has the broader definition of violence advocated above also made it more difficult to identify trends? The challenge remains in continuing to be able to measure just what is going on. It is only then that the need for particular policies and initiatives, as well as their progress and effectiveness, may become clearer (Walby et al. 2017).

Explaining violence

The accumulation of data referred to previously does not in itself provide clear answers as to why violence happens. Stanko's (2002) observation that there are far more statistics about violence than there is knowledge still rings true. Rakil, speaking in 2015 about domestic violence, asserted that the biggest question over the previous 25 years was trying to find how it could be explained.[3] This uncertainty would also apply across the continuum of common violence. Following detailed analyses and audits of a wide range of international studies and research, a helpful ecological perspective in seeking to explain common interpersonal violence has been put forward (WHO 2004). In summary, this approach presents the relationship between a complex mix of sociological, psychological and biological factors as having some explanatory power for violent behaviour. Each of these factors will now be explored in considering Simon's behaviour.

Sociological issues

At the time in question, it was regularly acknowledged that nowhere in Britain was child poverty more entrenched, reached greater depths or more concentrated than in Northern Ireland (Heenan and Birrell 2005). This was certainly Simon's experience in growing up in one of its most deprived and troubled areas. His community was beset with significant communal conflict; high levels of generational unemployment; poverty; poor housing; and associated physical and mental health problems. Such social deprivation and poverty has been associated with high levels of common violence, including the growth of gang-related and hate-motivated crimes (Walby 2009; WHO 2014).

Simon's wider cultural, socio-political context was also one in which patriarchal attitudes not only permitted, but actually promoted dominance of women by men (Devaney 2014). Various feminist analyses are helpful in explaining high levels of violence against women and children which occur within different sections and classes within societies and not just those that are socially deprived. I encountered negative and derisory attitudes towards women in the minds of a significant number of the men from across a range of backgrounds with whom I worked.[4]

Psychological issues

Simon's early family life involved several adversities, including witnessing and experiencing violence and criminality within his home. His parents, who separated, also had poor mental health and addiction issues. It is not possible to be precise as to how the impact of these multiple maltreatments and traumas directly influenced his future violent behaviour (Price-Robertson et al. 2011). However, they certainly played out negatively for him in terms of various attachment, developmental and relationship issues, and there is some evidence of an association between such factors and subsequent engagement in aggressive and antisocial behaviour (WHO 2014).

Some research suggests a more pronounced link between psychological adversities, mental health problems and substance misuse in relation to certain women for whom violent and aggressive behaviour becomes a problem. There appears to be a complex and overlapping prevalence of victimisation, household dysfunction, substance abuse and mental health issues as potential precursors for the future violence of certain women (Messina et al. 2007; Bair-Merritt et al. 2010).

Biological issues

That the different pathways into violence for men and women suggested in the previous point may also have some biological roots remains a controversial issue. To what extent are the greater rates of violence among men related to biological sex differences – an inbuilt feature of masculinity (Jones 2008)? There is, as yet, certainly no evidence of a male violence gene, or for that matter any violence gene. There is significant literature which does suggest the relevance of some genetic factors. For example, intellectual difficulties, psychopathy, as well as hormonal and dietary factors may be associated with some manifestations of aggression and violence. Simon had mild intellectual difficulties, and the limitations in his thinking may well have contributed in some degree to the subsequent violence that he used in his life. More recent developments within neuroscience are claiming to provide some explanation as to how the interplay between our experiences and our genes makes us who we are (Duckworth 2016).

Choice, responsibility and power

The ecological framework points up the interplay of individual, family, community, societal and cultural factors as throwing some light on Simon's journey into violence. Several significant elements in his life clearly resonate with the research reviewed above as being associated with his use of violence. Gerhardt (2004) memorably suggested that the genes may provide the raw material, but it is the cooking, particularly in infancy and in the inequalities in life, that counts.

The nature of Simon's complex biological, psychological and social mix and its precise relationship with his violence will always be elusive. It also raises fundamental questions about human freedom and choice. Did the above combination of factors take away Simon's ability to make his own behavioral choices (Houston 2015)? I often thought that if I had experienced similar circumstances maybe I would also have drifted into violence. However, I knew other young men from similar backgrounds and with other difficulties who did not. The social work values that will be explored in Chapter 3 respected Simon as a person with agency. The most essential parts of life, including the use of violence, are ultimately 'matters of individual responsibility and moral choice' (Brooks 2015). The situations within his life when Simon used violence were those in which he chose to use his personal power, as he did with Sarah and his mother.

The issue of power needs to be considered across the various manifestations of common violence. Whether violent and coercive acts are carried out by one partner against the other within an intimate relationship, by one family member against another, by a carer against a frail elderly relative, by a young person bullying a child at school, by an older man against a young person or by one gang member against another, they need to be considered within contexts of inequality and power (Milner and Myers 2016). Violence always seems to increase within situations of powerlessness and vulnerability. A striking and disturbing example of this reality is seen in a major review of 17 national studies which found that children with disabilities were nearly four times more likely to be victims of physical violence and nearly three times of sexual violence (UNICEF 2013). This also explains why many of those who use violence do so across a range of types of violence – the misuse of power is a common denominator.

Addressing common violence

The United Nations' goal to end violence, including gender-based violence, is articulated within its Sustainable Development Goals.[5] This is a recognition of the reality of the links between violence and inequalities. The paradox is that while the issue of power may have been fundamental to an understanding of Simon's violent lashing out, his decisions to abuse power should also be considered within the powerlessness and exclusion he experienced across many aspects of his life. As Pope Francis put it, until exclusion and inequality in society and between peoples are reversed, it will be impossible to eliminate violence.[6] Greater equality will be the best general antidote and most pressing need in addressing violence.

A broad and expansive range of tougher laws as well as preventative systemic responses to violence also continue to be brought forward to address common violence across the world (WHO 2014). The preventative strategies target the various sociological, psychological and biological roots of violence outlined in the previous section. These include various family- and parenting-based initiatives to help develop safer, more stable and nurturing relationships. For example, attention has been given to encouraging the important role fathers can play in helping their children not to become involved in violence. (Lewis and Lamb 2007). Other initiatives involve teaching life skills to children and adolescents, reducing the availability and harmful use of alcohol, reducing access to guns and knives, etc. Social work, in collaboration with many other stakeholders and communities, plays a role in such responses, in particular, within the critically important areas of victim identification, care and support (WHO 2014).

While acknowledging the above strategies, the focus for the remainder of this chapter is on the role of face-to-face interventions with those people who are actually using the violence. Not unreasonably, given some of the key themes already mentioned, a 'patriarchal' practice and policy paradigm has dominated much of the work in this area since the 1980s (Lazenbatt and Devaney 2016). Many of the interventions that have been developed have focused on the importance of challenging the beliefs, attitudes and expectations around male supremacy which have been viewed as underpinning much violence. This approach has been shown to make positive contributions to safety (Worrall et al. 2008; Kelly and Westmarland 2015).

At the same time, a 2013 survey of 54 European programmes working with men who had been violent within their intimate relationships highlighted that there was a wide disparity in the approaches to the work. Furthermore, the survey also identified limitations in the robustness of the evidence informing some of the programme designs (Hamilton et al. 2013).

Men who perpetrate domestic violence are a heterogeneous group. Simon used different types of violence; it was not just about his attitudes towards women, there were also other factors at play (Willman and Makisaka 2010). A large-scale review aimed at developing legitimate strategies for reducing the rates of violence against women in society argued for the need not only to address patriarchal views, but, critically, to also focus on other forms and levels of general violence. It concluded that helping people address the use of violence within their lives, both of a gender-based and non-gender-based nature, would not only help them become safer in general but would also keep women safer (Herrero et al. 2017).

There is a wide diversity in those who use violence within their relationships, families or communities and the ways in which the violence is used. The key point is that, whatever form it takes, the violent behaviour can be engaged with. Dialogue should take place with the person, exploring their social and cultural experiences, as well as their relevant psychological and emotional history. The dialogue can also be related to the person's goals, expectations, motivating attitudes and actions in seeking to promote and encourage more non-violent pathways (Jones 2008).

The issues around abuse of power, freedom of choice and responsibility will also be a critical part of face-to-face conversations and interventions. There is always the choice to use power positively. No one is ever 'done'; as far as being a final version of oneself, there is always the continuing possibility of choice and change (Peterson 2006). There is both space and a need for flexible and person-centred responses and dialogue to help someone address differing patterns of behaviour and motivations in relation to the use of violence in whatever form or forms it is manifested (Emmer 2011).

Conclusion

This chapter has sought to condense an overwhelming, conflicting and continually growing amount of statistical, research and evidence-informed theoretical perspectives in relation to the perennial violence problem. The complexity of the material demands that we content ourselves with a lesser understanding (Kilby 2013, p. 265). It is still the case that the various perspectives and 'theories' on violence remain 'somewhat under-informed by evidence' (Walby et al. 2017, p. 7). Consequently, the objectives set at the start of the chapter, namely to define, measure, explain and respond to common violence, have not been fully met.

Despite this, what can be said is that the problem of common violence is huge, it is a major health-related problem across the world and some people can be helped to move towards non-violence. This is ample justification for a strong social work response. Of course, there will always be significant risk issues, and these will receive further attention in Chapter 4. Allowing for that, the challenge now is to show precisely how a social work process, based on its values and knowledge, can offer a meaningful engagement with a person whose use of violence, in whatever form it takes, is causing difficulty. This is the task of the next chapter in continuing to lay the groundwork for the conversations promoting non-violence in Part II.

Notes

1 There are still concerns around child sexual exploitation; for example, the continuing traces of acceptance within some cultural contexts around the issue of child brides. Fr Cullen who has been a lifelong campaigner against the sexual abuse of children within the Philippines raised this continuing source of abuse in a speech he made to the Oireachtas Foreign Affairs Committee,The Republic of Ireland Government, in 2017.
   Another completely separate issue was reported in the Guardian online in June 2017. A review into compensation for children who had been sexually abused by the Criminal Injuries Compensation Authority in England identified almost 700 child victims who had not received compensation. Even though some of the people who had abused them had received custodial sentences, the children had been deemed in some way complicit in their abuse.
2 An online survey (Student Consent Research Collaboration) carried out by the Queens University Student Union in Belfast in 2017.
3 M Rakil speaking at the Inaugural European Conference on Domestic Violence at Queens University Belfast in 2015.
4 At the time of writing there is much concern as to the continuing abusive attitudes and actions that many women experience across different areas of life. For example, a 2017 BBC survey report on its News Channels into the British House of Commons described a 'sexist, laddisth and misogynistic culture where there was a toxic mix of alcohol and power'.
5 In 2015 the United Nations launched its 17 Sustainable Development Goals for 2030, including a commitment to strive towards peace and justice and equality.
6 Speech delivered by Pope Francis on 15 March 2013 during a meeting of world cardinals in which he attacked the inequalities within the global economic system that were 'spawning violence'.

References

Alvarez, A. and Bachman, R. (2013) *Violence The Enduring Problem* (2nd edition). London: Sage.
Bair-Merritt, M.H., Crowne, S.S., Thompson, D. A. et al. (2010) Why Do Women Use Intimate Partner Violence? A Systematic Review of Women's Motivations. *Trauma Violence Abuse*. 11: 178–189.
Brison, S. (2002) *Aftermath: Violence and the Remaking of Self.* Princeton, NJ: Princeton University Press.
Brooks, D. (2015) *The Road to Character.* London: Penguin.
Buzi, R.S., Smith, P.B., Kozinetz, C.A. and Wiemann, C.M. (2017) Pregnant Adolescents As Perpetrators and Victims of Intimate Partner Violence. *Journal of Interpersonal Violence*, 20 April 20.

Cismaru, M. and Lavack, A.M. (2011) Campaigns Targeting Perpetrators of Intimate Partner Violence. *Trauma, Violence, and Abuse*, 12(4): 183–197.

Devaney, J. (2014) Male Perpetrators of Domestic Violence: How Should We Hold Them to Account. *The Political Quarterly*, 85(4), October to December

Duckworth, A. (2016) *Grit the Power of Passion and Perseverance*. London: Vermillion.

Emmer, C. (2011) Disorder or Deviant Order? Re-theorising Domestic Violence in Terms of Order, Power and Legitimacy. *A Typology Aggression and Violent Behaviour*, 16(6): 525–540.

Evason, E. (1982) *Hidden Violence: A Study of Battered Women in Northern Ireland*. Belfast: Farset Co-operative Press.

Fisher, B.S., Zink, T. and Regan, S.L. (2010) Abuses against Older Women: Prevalence and Health Effects. *Abstract Journal of Interpersonal Violence*, 20(10): 1–15.

FRA European Union Agency for Fundamental Rights (2014) *Violence against Women: An EU-wide Survey*. Luxemburg: Publications Office of the EU.

Gerhardt, S. (2004) *Why Love Matters: How Affection Shapes a Baby's Brain*. East Sussex: Routledge.

Hamilton, L., Koehler, J. A. & Losel, F. A. (2013) Domestic Violence Perpetrator Programmes in Europe, Part 1: A Survey of Current Practice. *International Journal of Offender Therapy and Comparative Criminology*, 57(10).

Harne, L. and Radford, J. (2008) *Tackling Domestic Violence: Theories, Policies and Practice*. Maidenhead: Open University Press.

Keenan, D. and Birrell, D. (2015) *Social Work in Norther Ireland: Conflict and Change*. University of Bristol: Policy Press.

Herrero, J., Torres, A., Rodríguez, F.J. and Juarros-Basterretxea, J. (2017) Intimate Partner Violence against Women in the European Union: The Influence of Male Partners' Traditional Gender Roles and General Violence. *Psychology of Violence* © 2017, 7(3): 385.

Houston, S. (2015) *Reflective Practice: A Model for Supervision and Practice in Social Work*. Belfast: NISCC.

Jones, D.W. (2008) *Understanding Criminal Behaviour: Psychosocial Approaches to Criminality*. Cullompton: Willan.

Jones, R. (2011) Violence Perpetrated by Young People against Their Parents: Issues and Recommendations for Service Provision. Presentation to Domestic Violence Special Interest Group, Queens University Belfast.

Kamimura, A., Nourian, M., Assasnik, N., Rathi, N. and Franchek-Roa, K. (2017) The Use of Physical Violence Against Intimate Partners by Female College Students in India. *Violence and Gender*, 4(1): 11–16.

Kelly, L. and Westmarland, N. (2015) *Domestic Violence Perpetrator Programmes: Steps Towards Change*. Project Mirabal Final Report. London and Durham: London Metropolitan University and Durham University.

Kilby, J. (2013) Theorising Violence. *European Journal of Social Theory*, 16(3): 261–272. Available at https://doi.org/10.1177/1368431013476579.

Lazenbatt, A. and Devaney, J. (2016) *Domestic Violence Perpetrators: Evidence Informed Responses*. London: Routledge

Lewis, C. and Lamb, M.E. (2007) *Understanding Fatherhood: A Review of Recent Research*. London: Joseph Roundtree Foundation.

Lloyd, T. (2009) *Stuck in the Middle (Some Young Men's Experiences of Violence, Conflict & Safety)*. Centre for Young Men's Studies. University of Ulster Publications.

Lovestad, S. and Krantz, G., (2015) Men and Women's Exposure and Perpetration of Partner Violence: An Epidemiological Study from Sweden. Paper presented to the First European Conference, Belfast.

McWilliams, M. and McKiernan, J. (1993) *Bringing it out into the Open: Domestic Violence in Northern Ireland*. Belfast: HMSO.

Messina, N., Grella, C., Burdon, W. et al. (2007) Childhood Adverse Events and Current Traumatic Distress: A Comparison of Men and Women Prisoners. *Criminal Justice Behaviour*, 34: 1385–1401.

Milner, J. and Myers, S. (2016) *Working with Violence and Confrontation Using Solution Focused Approaches*. London: Jessica Kingsley.

Musson, P. (2017) *Making Sense of Theory and its Application to Social Work Practice*. St Albans: Critical Publishing.

Peterson, C. (2006) *A Primer in Positive Psychology*. New York: Open University Press.

Pinker, S. (2012) *The Better Angels of Our Nature*. London: Penguin.

Price-Robertson, R., Rush, P., Wall, L. and Higgins, D. (2011) Rarely an Isolated Incident: Acknowledging the Interrelatedness of Child Maltreatment, vVictimisation and Trauma. Australian Institute of Family Studies.

Stanko, E.A. (2002) *Taking Stock: What Do We Know about Interpersonal Violence?* London: Economic and Social Research Council.

UNICEF (2013) *The State of the World's Children: Children with Disabilities*. New York: United Nations Children's Fund. Available at pubdoc@unicef.org www.unicef.org/sowc2013.

Walby, S. (2009) *Globalisation and Inequalities*. London: Sage.

Walby, S., Towers, J., Balderston, S.,.Corradi, C., Francis, B., Heiskanen, M., Helweg-Larsen, K., Mergaert, L., Olive, P., Palmer, E.,.Stöckl, H. and Strid, S. (2017) *The Concept and Measurement of Violence against Women and Men*. Bristol: Policy Press.

Willman, A. and Makisaka, M. (2010) Interpersonal Violence Prevention: A Review of the Evidence and Emerging Lessons. World Development Report Background Paper.

World Health Organisation (2002) *World Report on Violence and Health: A Summary*. Geneva: WHO.

World Health Organisation (2004) *Preventing Violence: An Agenda to Implementing the Recommendations of the World Report on Violence and Health*. Geneva: WHO.

World Health Organisation (2014) *Global Statistics Report on Violence Prevention*. Geneva: WHO.

Worrall, A., Boylan, J. and Roberts, D. (2008) Children's and Young People's Experiences of Domestic Violence Involving Adults in a Parenting Role. SCIE Research Briefing 25.

Zink, T., Jacobson, C.J., Regan, S. and Pabst, S. (2004). Hidden Victims: Older Women with Intimate Partner Violence and Their Health Care Experiences and Needs. *Journal of Women's Health*, 13: 898–906.

Chapter 3

Social work and violence

Introduction

The President of the International Federation of Social Workers has spoken of the journey that many social workers have to travel, with both the victims and the perpetrators of violence.[1] Her words reflect the reality that social work often involves engagement with those for whom the use of common violence is a difficult issue. She reaffirmed and challenged the profession to continue to try to understand and prevent such violence. Social work practice needs to take account of and learn from the material covered in the previous chapters. It should place itself within the comprehensive multi-faceted responses that view common violence as an important public health, social well-being, criminal justice, development and gender issue.

This chapter will concentrate on how this is done, focusing on the person-centred social work process itself; specifically, its commitment to its core values, and the use of its knowledge base, in addressing the use of violence with the individual. This process can allow for an appropriate response across the wide range of behaviours that are contained within the definition of common violence. Once again, Simon will provide the starting point in bringing to life the social work contribution.

Example 7 The social work process, violence and Simon

When he was 19 years old, Simon received a one-year Probation Order in respect of various offences, including assault. Once again, and not for the last time, I was back in his life, as his Probation Officer, taking forward a social work intervention with him. In doing this, I needed to gain an understanding of and empathy for the various circumstances, history, difficulties and challenges he faced, as outlined in Chapter 2.

At this time, Simon was becoming increasingly involved in criminal and antisocial behaviour, often fuelled by his increasing reliance on alcohol. His moderate learning difficulty also contributed to some impulsive and poor decision-making. There were also positives. I knew from my previous involvement that he was a popular young person, and well-liked by friends and family members. I remember his grandmother, who I met on a few occasions when visiting the family home, describing him as someone with 'a good heart but easily led'. He was loyal to those he cared about. He did have some sense of what was right and what was wrong. He maintained positive relationships with some of the women in his life, particularly with his grandmother and one of his older sisters.

As an alternative to custody, Simon indicated that he was prepared to deal with issues in his life that were causing difficulty both for him and for others. In our assessment, Simon and I were able to agree three priorities. These focused on accessing more positive educational, vocational and leisure opportunities, reducing his intake of alcohol, and moving to non-violence. A purposeful and planned response was put in place to work towards the above goals. In other words, I sought to take forward a social work process with Simon that was both person centred and holistic.

With varying degrees of success, I worked with him in taking tiny positive steps that would contribute to his overall personal and social well-being. Even minor positive developments (for example, getting a little more structure into his life and taking part in enjoyable diversionary activities) indirectly had a positive impact on the amount of violence he got involved in. However, the attention to broader needs did not preclude the necessity to prioritise the issue of Simon's use of violence itself and all its implications and consequences. This also needed to be a key element within the agreed social work process, and the focus for the remainder of this chapter will be on how social work values and knowledge were applied specifically in this regard.

Human rights, social justice, social work values and violence

Ultimately, social work is a social rights and justice profession (Munroe 2011). As already described in Chapter 1, Simon was part of a community that had experienced generational poverty, inequality and discrimination. The people who lived in the community were often subject to stereotypical and derogatory judgement. As a senior civil servant reported in an internal memo at the time, 'a large section of the population is alienated from the institutions of government and indeed, in some respects, from normal civilised behaviour'.[2] I had to guard against the presence of such negative stereotyping making its way into my practice. Even though there was little I could do at the time about the prevailing social inequalities experienced by Simon, at the very least I sought to remain sensitive to their impact. My agency's ongoing commitment to community development initiatives, referred to in Chapter 1, demonstrated a solidarity with the community in which Simon lived.

Stereotyping could also prevail in other ways. The research material in Chapter 2 raised the issue of different pathways into violence between men and women. This needed to be treated with care, and critically considered. There was, and remains, a danger of a mind-set that, to oversimplify it, may see men who were violent as 'bad' and needing punishment and women as 'mad' and needing therapy (Milner and Myers 2016). There was, and remains, the danger of generalising characteristics as if they were part and parcel of being a man or woman. I viewed Simon, and each person, as an individual full of the spirit of life (Chittister 2015). This reflected the four core social work values underpinning my practice.

First, I respected Simon as a person, with a unique, mysterious complexity and inherent, irreducible dignity (Brooks 2015). This respect depended neither on how he behaved, his usefulness nor his likeability (Banks 2006).

Second, I sought to ensure not only his protection and safety, but also that of others. Unlike respect, we see later how Simon's behaviour did impact upon the way this value played out.

Third, I accepted his right to choice and self-determination. I could never pretend to be in an equal relationship with him. As his Probation Officer I had significant power and authority invested in my role. Nevertheless, I sought to work in partnership with him to achieve mutual understanding and agreed pro-social goals that would be beneficial to himself and to others (Turnell and Edwards 1999).

Fourth, I endeavoured to work with Simon in ways that were evidence informed in terms of what would be most likely to contribute to his social well-being as well as to those with whom he had relationships. This was challenging and involved continuously promoting pro-social attitudes and actions with Simon and accessing positive opportunities and experiences within a positive and affirming relationship.

The above core values reflect the four guiding principles that Banks (2006) identified in her research into ethical codes used by social workers in 30 different countries. They reflect beliefs about what is worthy and valued in the nature of a good life and a good society and what should be the drivers for social work practice (Doel 2016). They are very broad principles about which it would be difficult to find disagreement. However, given various ethical tensions, their application can be open to quite disparate interpretation (Shardlow 2013). This is particularly so when working with the issue of violence and was certainly the case in my work with Simon.

In preparing a report for the court, my agency required me to refer to Simon as an offender or perpetrator. This was immediately at odds with my commitment to respecting his dignity by making the simple but important gesture to acknowledge him by the use of his name. Language 'can elevate and inspire or demonise and destroy' (Saleebey 2012, p. 11). Simon's use of violence did not reflect his entire identity. If terms or labels are required, is it not preferable to develop those that have a different perspective? For example, in the area of sexual abuse, Milner and Myers (2016) suggest that language such as 'children with sexually harmful or concerning behaviours' or 'young people with sexually problematic behaviours' is more appropriate. This refocuses on the unwanted behaviour rather than on the young person. It is not the person who is the problem; it is the behaviour. 'Why call someone by what we don't want them to be?'[3] (Willis 2018).

I also experienced a challenging value tension in seeking to work in partnership with Simon, while at the same time recognising the importance of protection and justice for those whose human rights he had violated. On one occasion I was left with a difficult decision, having observed his use of violence against another person. I decided to share this information with the police. I told Simon my reasons for doing so and, even though he objected, I proceeded, and it ultimately led to a conviction and a period in custody. Another colleague subsequently indicated to me that they would have come to a contrasting conclusion, and not have risked damaging my relationship with Simon. In working with the issue of violence, the commitment to justice and to the values identified above will not avoid difficult choices having to be made, an issue that will be revisited in Chapter 4 on risk.

Social Work Knowledge and Violence

Trevithick (2012) rightly points out that the knowledge base for social work is wide and ever-changing as the profession continues to stretch itself across an expanding range of situations. This is particularly the case when responding appropriately to a person's use of violence. However, change and continuity can go together. Relationship-based social work has been an unchanging and vital foundation to my practice throughout my career across many settings. A significant body of professional and academic literature continues to recognise its contribution to practice (Mc Colgan and Mc Mullan 2017). This was at the heart of my practice with Simon. I formed and fostered an empathic relationship with him. I wanted to make it as safe as possible for him to engage in talking and thinking about difficult issues in his life, including his use of violence.

The importance of relationship, particularly in working with the issue of violence, was further reinforced for me by Braithwaite's (1989) emerging theory of re-integrative shaming. This helped me recognise the constant danger that I could, all too easily, in subtle or other ways, shame and condemn Simon as a person who bullied and sought to control others. Such an approach ran the risk of reinforcing his sense of identity as a violent person and was likely to produce nothing more than a defiant reaction. Of course, this did not mean that the damage his use of violence did was downplayed, ignored, nor the consequences not dealt with. Neither did it mean that there were no issues of shame to be dealt with. However, I tried to do this in a way that sought to value Simon the person, his views, beliefs, goals, difficulties, etc. and in continually encouraging him to move towards non-violence.

I also needed to integrate relationship-based practice with other theoretical perspectives to inform and give further direction to my intervention with Simon. In particular, informed by a cognitive behavioural approach, I encouraged Simon to reflect more on some of his violent actions and whether he could see their relationship with some of his thinking or with his emotions. Such an approach reflected the practice of the Probation Service in Northern Ireland at the time which was developing a range of mainly cognitive behavioural-inspired interventions.

These approaches have now been implemented globally, mainly with adults but also with young people, and have been demonstrated as altering thinking processes associated with violence (Goldstein et al. 2004). Indeed, they are relevant and appropriate in helping people change various aspects of their behaviour. As Pinker (2012) put it, we can all benefit from addressing the quirks in cognitive and emotional make-up which gives rise to a substantial proportion of avoidable human misery.

However, at the time I was working with Simon, it was also becoming clear that cognitive behavioural-inspired interventions were not always effective in themselves. For some of those on the receiving end, it felt as if they were being offered and even pressurised into a 'solution' to something which, in the first place, they did not fully accept was a problem for them. The emergence of motivational interviewing helped address this issue. First, it recognised and indeed welcomed denial and resistance as understandable. These may be about warding off judgements from others, trying to avoid acceptance of a label of being a violent person or protecting self-esteem. They are not always necessarily factors that increase the risk of future violence (Marshall 2009). Described as person centered, but with an edge, motivational interviewing recognises this reality. It encourages the person to reflect on whether, from their own perspective, there is any discrepancy or tension between current aspects of their behaviour and their important life goals (Miller and Rollnick 2002). The person's reasons for wanting to do something about any aspect of behaviour, or, in other words, the 'why' question need to be addressed first. This is reflected in the focus of the first conversation in Part II. It is only then that the question of 'what' needs to be done may be taken forward.

As well as motivational interviewing, there have been other significant developments that have helped me continue to refine and enhance my practice since I worked with Simon. In particular, the growth of positive psychology has made significant contributions (Seligman 2011). Strengths based and resilience perspectives have further encouraged movement away from a negative, deficit-oriented form of practice to one that seeks out positives, no matter how small or hidden, and also seeks to place this in the context of a person's environment. Similarly, narrative and solution-focused approaches have also emphasised the importance of listening to the person's own first-hand account of their life and the place of violence within it.

Importantly, they also recognise that the person will know more about their violence than will any practitioner. As with other areas of practice we can learn from those who are using violence about what may be causing it and what may help prevent it (Gilligan 1998). This encourages the adoption of a 'not-knowing' stance towards the person and for the worker to remain curious and to continue to ask questions, rather than closing down the conversations with 'the answer' (Milner and Myers 2016).

Educational and coaching-inspired approaches also continue to be helpful in providing specific guidance to individuals in dealing with challenging situations or giving feedback on how the person may have dealt with a particularly provocative or conflictual situation that may trigger a violent reaction from them. This was particularly relevant for Simon in terms of his mild learning difficulties and the importance of helping his understanding. However, in the spirit of motivational interviewing, advice should be offered rather than imposed upon the individual.

The depth and breadth of the continuously evolving theoretical knowledge, which will inform the conversations outlined in Part II of this volume, is daunting. Neither is there the space to do justice to each of the substantial theoretical perspectives mentioned above and which are being drawn upon. The application of each relevant theory will present challenges, namely how and when to use it appropriately and avoid the danger of a muddled intervention with the sense of 'just throwing the kitchen sink' at the issue of a person's violence.

This eclecticism needs to be thought through and articulated. It also needs to fit within an approach which remains flexible and allows for fluidity in this type of work. The worker should never feel that they are in a straitjacket but have discretion when responding appropriately to each individual and their particular needs and to issues as they arise. To this end, further material in relation to the specific application of the various perspectives will be incorporated into the guidance for the conversations outlined throughout Part II.

The challenges of practice

The Munroe Report (2011) highlighted the pressures on frontline social work coming together to create a defensive system that puts so much emphasis on procedures and recording. This issue will be returned to in the Chapter 4, but for now, one of its consequences is that insufficient attention is given to developing and supporting the expertise to work effectively with those individuals who may be using violence.

I have experienced periods when carrying an excessive and 'high-risk' case load has pressurised me into practice that was becoming increasingly procedural and informationally driven. Unfortunately, the reality of such bureaucratic responses is to take us further away from engaging with the complexities of violence, risk and uncertainty that should be the business of social work (Ruch 2013; Scragg 2013). It certainly makes it difficult to take forward the more relational approach to working with those for whom the use of violence is a problem advocated above and presented in Part II.

I continue to have encounters with practice situations where there is insignificant or meaningless engagement with the person who has been using violence. I have also been aware of occasions when there is significant communication in ways that can sometimes be unhelpful. I have observed approaches that involve direct confrontation of what are viewed as the various defences of those using violence in seeking to jolt the person into active behaviour change. Sometimes such an approach is taken within case conferences with a 'resistant' parent and in some group work practices. While continuing to have its advocates, in my experience a frequent outcome of such an approach has been resistance or disguised compliance (Forrester et al. 2008).

A report prepared for the Centre of Social Justice found some evidence of a lack of motivation and skills across various services to engage with abusive fathers (Farmer and Callan 2012). Recommendations included that there was a need for further training and development of particular skills by social workers in engaging with domestically abusive fathers as well as with couples where violence is mutual. The messages contained in this publication are applicable across the different types of common violence and are relevant to this need.

Character contests

As both a residential and community social worker, I often had to address outbursts of violence which a person I was working with was continuing to perpetrate in the course of their life. These were often unpredictable, as in the memorable example recounted below.

Example 8 The pink gloves!

I was participating in a football match between two groups of young men from across the communal divide in Northern Ireland. This was part of the initiative mentioned in Chapter 1 (p. 15) involving a range of activities exploring issues around dealing with difference and promoting mutual respect. It was a beautiful cold winter's day, and everyone was looking forward to the game. As both teams were running out onto the pitch from the changing rooms, one player was wearing a pair of pink gloves. Almost immediately someone from the opposing team yelled out, 'Look at that queer with his pink gloves.' In an instant, the young man wearing the gloves shouted back across the pitch, 'That's not what your girl was saying last night when I was rubbing them all over her.' (He used more colourful language with reference to various anatomical features which I will not repeat.) Amid the laughter, the young man who had made the opening statement started to run towards the other party. All the while a two-way abusive verbal interaction continued between them. Both parties clearly interpreted each other's statements and body language as offensive. It was soon obvious that they both also perceived the confrontation as being of a nature that required an aggressive and violent response. Within seconds, they started to fight viciously without any thought for the possible consequences.

The oppressive attitudes which underpinned the verbal abuse were explored with the young men in subsequent meetings and will not be addressed here. The focus will be on the event as an illustration of the violence-related phenomenon described many years ago by Luckenbill (1977) as character contests. These interactions will be encountered by many social workers. The key issue is the loss of face or humiliation that a person experiences. The remark about the gloves was the 'opening round' in the 'contest' which led to violence. As the two young men traded jibes and insults, the resultant loss of self-esteem that they experienced has been described as almost being akin to the death or destruction of self and their individual identity (Gilligan 2000). In such moments the person will do anything to protect this, particularly in front of the watching audience.

Fortunately, in the example above, the violence was quickly contained. However, Musson (2017) presents a tragic example in which Bailey Gwynne, a 16-year-old boy, was stabbed and killed by a fellow pupil over what started as an argument about a biscuit that led to a taunt about being overweight. Such a phenomenon can also occur within relationships and families, where the most serious violence erupts from an apparently minor issue. Musson argues that educating young people about coping with this emotional arousal and hijacking, particularly around loss of face, shame and anger, should be part of the school curriculum. The degree to which an individual can be helped to regulate their emotional arousal within such challenging contexts should also be something with which social workers in many settings should engage. It is a key theme within several of the conversations in Part II of this volume.

As already stated in the introduction (see p. 5), this publication will not focus on how to intervene when such outbursts take place, nor on the necessary debriefing and processing that should happen as soon after the outburst as possible.

Conclusion

I have used the example of Simon in this chapter to place in context some of the social work conversations that were to take place with him in regard to his use of violence. Of course, the nature of these conversations has continued to develop over the years. Those that will be presented in Part II of this volume have evolved from many previous interventions for which I have been responsible and witnessed across a wide array of common violence situations within relationships, families and communities. They represent the culmination of the work that has taken place within the Probation Service, the Youth Justice Agency, various health and social care statutory agencies, the Voluntary Sector as well as within independent practice across Northern Ireland.

Crucially, the Northern Ireland Probation Service, which has developed much of this practice, continues to recognise the critical importance of social work as its professional foundation. Unlike its sister organisation in England, it resisted a move away from social work values and rehabilitative ideals. It was determined to avoid becoming what would possibly be nothing more than a centralised, politicised agency of social control and enforcement (Whitehead and Stratham 2006).

The current internationally agreed definition of social work and UK National Occupational Standards (UKCES 2011) both highlight that the social work profession is about problem-solving in human relationships. Common violence is a problem in human relationships. Contributing to helping a person solve the problem of their use of violence within their lives, in whatever ways this is manifested, is the business of social work. This will involve dialogue. The conversations in Part II are offered as a contribution to this dialogue in helping a person begin to address whatever manifestations of violence are disfiguring their lives. These conversations should be part of everyday social work practice.

Finally, face-to-face social work practice always needs to recognise that violence and risk co-exist. Taking forward the social work conversations in a way that acknowledges and addresses the ever-present reality of risk is the major challenge for the final chapter in Part I.

Notes

1 Ruth Stark, the then President of the International Federation of Social Workers, was speaking in memory of Christine Archibald, a social worker who had devoted her professional life to working with homeless people and who was one of 11 people killed (8 victims and 3 attackers) in a terrorist attack on London Bridge on 4 June 2017.
2 Brian Feeney is a political commentator in Northern Ireland and reported this statement having been made in the official papers which were released for public viewing in 2017.

3 Language is important. I remember being involved in criminal justice teaching on one of the social work training programmes in Northern Ireland and making the suggestion that the name for the module 'Social Work with Offenders' would be more appropriately called 'Social Work within the Criminal Justice System'. More recently, I welcomed the decision of a previously named 'Young Offenders Centre' to be renamed as a college and the young people who were sent there to be referred to as students rather than as offenders.

References

Banks, S. (2006) *Ethics and Values in Social Work*. Basingstoke: Palgrave Macmillan.
Braithwaite, J. (1989) *Crime, Shame and Re-integration*. Cambridge: Cambridge University Press.
Brooks, D. (2015) *The Road to Character*. Harmondsworth: Penguin.
Chittister, J. (2015) *The Gift of Years: Growing Older Gracefully*. London: Darton, Longman and Todd.
Doel, M. (2016) *Rights and Wrongs in Social Work*. London: Palgrave.
Farmer, E. and Callan, S. (2012) *Beyond Violence London: Breaking Cycles of Domestic Abuse*. London: The Centre for Social Justice.
Forrester, D., Kershaw, S., Moss, H. and Hughes, L. (2008) Communication Skills in Child Protection: How Do Social Workers Talk to Parents? *Child and Family Social Work*, 13: 41–51.
Gilligan, J. (2000) *Violence: Reflections on our Deadliest Epidemic*. London: Jessica Kingsley.
Goldstein, A.P., Glick, B. and Gibbs, J.C. (2004) *New Perspectives on Aggression Replacement Training: Practice Research and Application*. Chichester: Wiley & Sons.
Luckenbill, D.F. (1977) Criminal Homicide as a Situated Transaction. *Social Problems*, 25(2): 176–186.
Marshall, W.L. (2009). Self-esteem, Shame, Cognitive Distortions and Empathy in Sexual Offenders: Their Integration and Treatment Implications. *Psychology, Crime & Law*, 15(2 and 3): 217–234.
Mc Colgan, M. and Mc Mullan, C. (2017) *Doing Relationship Based Social Work: A Practical Guide to Building Relationships and Enabling Change*. London: Jessica Kingsley.
Miller, R.W. and Rollnick, S. (2002) *Motivational Interviewing Preparing People for Change*. London: The Guilford Press.
Milner, J. and Myers, S. (2016) *Working with Violence and Confrontation Using Solution Focused Approaches*. London: Jessica Kingsley.
Munroe, E. (2011) *The Munroe Review of Child Protection: Final Report A child-centred System*. London: The Stationery Office.
Musson, P. (2017) *Making Sense of Theory and its Application to Social Work Practice*. St Albans: Critical Publishing.
Pinker, S. (2012) *The Better Angels of Our Nature*. London: Penguin.
Ruch, G. (2013) Understanding Contemporary Social Work: We Need to Talk More about Relationships. In Parker, J. and Doel, M., *Professional Social Work*. London: Learning Matters.
Saleebey, D. (2012) Power in the People. In Saleebey, D. (ed.), *The Strengths Perspective in Social Work Practice* (3rd edition). Boston, MA: Allyn & Bacon.

Scrag, T. (2013) Working with your Manager. In Knott, C. and Scragg, T. (eds), *Reflective Practice in Social Work*. London: Learning Matters.
Seligman, M. (2011) *Flourish: A Visionary New Understanding of Happiness and Wellbeing*. New York: Simon & Schuster.
Shardlow, S.M. (2013) Ethical Tensions in Social Work. In Parker, J. and Doel, M., *Professional Social Work*. London: Learning Matters.
Trevithick, P. (2012) *Social Work Skills and Knowledge: A Practice Handbook*. Berkshire: Open University Press.
UKCES (2011) *National Occupational Standards for Social Work*. London: United Kingdom Commission for Education and Skills.
Whitehead, P. and Stratham, R. (2006) *The History of Probation: Politics, Power and Cultural Change 1876–2005*. London: Sweet & Maxwell.
Willis, G.M. (2018) Why Call Someone By What We Don't Want Them to Be? The Ethics of Labelling in Forensic/Correctional Psychology. *Psychology, Crime & Law*. DOI: 10.1080/1068316X.2017.1421640

Chapter 4

Risk and violence

Introduction

One of my earliest memories from practice was advocating for a young person in residential care to be allowed to spend more time at home. My optimistic outlook, particularly within the context of our positive relationship, distorted my perspective on risk. I lost sight of the fact that the relationship on its own was not a sufficient basis upon which to make judgements in regard to future risks of violence within his family situation.

It was only through listening to the views of other social workers more involved with the family situation that I became more sensitive to the real risks that were present. This chapter will focus on the need to ensure that, unlike my practice with the young person above, the conversations outlined in part II of this volume both fit within, and contribute to, the requirement to assess and manage the risk that always accompany a person's use of violence.

The unpredictability of violence and measuring risk

The limits to our understanding of violence have been a key theme thus far. It will never be possible to be absolutely certain as to the specific risk that a particular person may present through their future use of violence. The assumption that 'there is a clear divide between people who are violent and those who are not' is flawed (Milner and Myers 2016). As Maya Angelou said, 'I am capable of what every other human being is capable of. This is one of the great lessons of war and life.'[1] There is an unpredictability about violence that always needs to be remembered.

I have worked with people who I thought would be very violent and who were not, and vice versa. An extreme example of an unforeseen act of violence occurred while this book was being written and is outlined below.

While acknowledging the reality of human uncertainty, there has been considerable progress made in making better judgements and decisions in

Example 9 Unpredictable violence

On 12 May 2016, Mr Mathew Scully-Hickey was formally approved as an adoptive parent of an 18-month-old girl, Elsie. During the period up until his approval he was the subject of a comprehensive assessment and every aspect of his life was scrutinised in what is a necessarily invasive process. In particular, close attention was paid to various research-based violence-related factors that will be returned to later in this chapter. It was established that he had no history of violence. In addition, there were no concerns raised in the professional judgements of those involved in the case who worked closely with him for over a year in completing the assessment. He was assessed as being safe. The serious case review subsequently highlighted that there were missed opportunities to raise safeguarding issues and initiate child protection procedures during the period the child was living with Mr Scully - Hickey. Perhaps there was an over reliance on the lack of violence in his personal history. This may have contributed to an initial, overly positive assessment and a resultant failure to ensure a continuing professional engagement with the situation. Tragically, in July 2017, within two weeks of his approval and in what the court later described as a sudden and unpremeditated outburst of frustration, Mr Scully-Hickey killed the child and was convicted of her murder.

relation to risk and violence issues. Reference has previously been made to the widespread adoption of a public health model in taking forward preventative strategies to reduce the level of violence within society (Esbensen et al. 2009). A personal health issue reinforced for me the usefulness of a medical approach in considering risk and violence.

Some time ago and following a medical check-up and referral to the cancer department at my local hospital, I was informed that I had prostate cancer. After consultations with two specialists, I was given a choice of two options. One consultant recommended an intrusive medical procedure with significant side effects. The other proposed that my condition be actively monitored and to hold off on any invasive interventions with all the negative side effects that went with them. After much consideration, I decided to delay immediate treatment and put my trust in the consultant who felt there was every possibility that I would die with the condition but not from it. At the time of writing this, more than five years later, and hopefully without tempting fate, I can say that this appears to have been a reasonable decision.

In my conversations with the consultants, I got a sense that they were working with three very general categories of risk. First, those people whose condition was 'high risk' (that is, so far advanced and serious that drastic intervention was required and, even with that, the prospects were not good). Second, those people whose condition was well established, there was significant risk but there remained the possibility of an effective intervention and reduction of future risk. Third, a future low-risk category in response to which a limited or even a non-intervention was a reasonable decision. The more I listened to the consultants, the more similarities I noticed with my own struggles as a social worker in making judgements about the risks of someone continuing to use serious violence. At the same time, I could also see that the same general categories of risk were useful in addressing this challenge.

High risk of future violence

Peter was the third young man in the photograph mentioned in the introduction. Following a childhood marked by maltreatment, victimisation and trauma, both within his family and also within the context of the communal violence, he embarked on a pathway that involved increasingly harsher and more violent forms of masculinity (Mariani et al. 2017; Mathews et al. 2011). He became a member of a paramilitary gang, one of a 'frightening, fearless fraternity of criminal hard men' (Campbell 1993, p. 50). He physically abused and abandoned several young women and their children. His behaviour described to me by one of his partners sounded like a form of 'patriarchal terrorism'. He continued to use violence, despite various interventions in his life. His actions fitted those who have been described as 'life course persistent' perpetrators of violence (Moffitt 1993), and only ended when he was the victim of gang violence himself. His extreme level of violence may also have been associated with the presence of some other relevant factors in his life that have been associated with a high violence risk. These include hostility, impulsivity, substance abuse, major mental disorders, and antisocial or psychopathic personality factors (Serin and Preston 2001; Dutton 1998).

In Chapter 1, I referred to my previous work with men who had committed sexual offences against children. I still remember being initially shocked at the extraordinary level of deviousness demonstrated by a small number of these men. They could be manipulative and had the ability to lie convincingly (Travers 1999). One major study and evaluation of a cognitive behaviourally based UK programme delivered to such people in prison showed little or no changes in sexual and non-sexual re-offending, and in some cases there was an increase in risk of offending (Mews et al. 2017). Across different manifestations of violence, the reality is that there will be those (albeit very small in number) who will persist in using dangerous levels of common violence.

Medium risk of future violence

Simon's violence was never as serious or as frequent as that of Peter. He did not demonstrate the pervasive pattern of disregard for and violation of the rights of others within his relationships, family and wider afield in the community that

Peter did (Pinker 2012). He never considered carrying a knife or other weapons. As mentioned previously, he had positive relationships with his grandmother and sister. Unlike some of Peter's previous girlfriends, who were in fear of him – when I listened to Sarah she told me that she never had a real fear of Simon, she could give as good as she got – he just needed to sort out his drinking.

Simon did present risk, and I often had concerns in relation to his growing involvement in different aspects of violence at particular times. However, it was possible to address his use of violence with him. There was a sense that he was not happy with it, was open to change and that he fitted within a more medium continuum of risk. I have also worked with a range of people across different areas of violence who fitted within such a category. Chapter 2 presented some of the evidence that it is possible to intervene and help some people get safer, even within the most challenging area of domestic violence (Kelly and Westmarland 2015).

Low risk of future violence

Sarah used some violence against both Simon and her child. It was of a different nature and in my view fitted within a lower category of risk. She was devoted to her daughter and was ultimately able to put the child's needs first. She came to recognise the growing dangers of Simon's drinking, the resultant high-conflict nature of their relationship and the real danger that at times it could go beyond the 'throwing of a few plates'. Their relationship did not survive and she was able to move forward positively with her life.

Similarly, my own experience as well as the literature also shows evidence of significant numbers of young people being able to move away from community- or family-based violence as they mature (Jones 2008; Masson 2004). A significant number of men who have been involved in domestic violence appear to cease their behaviour without any apparent sanction or formal intervention (Devaney 2014). I have worked with people whose relationship with violence has been transient or context specific and, for one reason or another, have moved away from the significant use of violence.

Assessing the risk of future violence

The judgements I made in relation to the risk of future violence from Peter, Simon and Sarah were based on a combination of my professional judgement and reference to standardised violence-related assessment tools emerging from research (Barlow et al. 2012). These tools have become more sophisticated over the years, although at their core there has always been an analysis of what is known about a person's violent behaviour, in particular, its onset, its precise nature, its seriousness, how far it extends across different areas of the person's life, and its frequency and pattern. Awareness of these factors supported a technical and calculative approach to analysing the violence of Peter, James and Sarah I was able to see that Peter's violent behaviour was likely to have a continuity, beginning before adolescence and continuing into adulthood (Hemphill et al. 2009). Similarly, the relative stability of the manifestations of his violence was indicative of a high probability of future violence (Jones et al. 2010).

Alongside this actuarial approach, my professional judgement was also required. Probably more so in the cases of Simon and Sarah, this involved the many interactions I had with them, including some of the conversations in Part II. It also included significant engagement with their families, those on the receiving end of the violence, as well as others within their community and subsequent reflections with colleagues in supervision.

Working with the categories of risk

The risk categories are helpful. However, they are not completely distinct entities. They will always be fluid and will merge into each other. There are both categories and also a continuum. There is never certainty. My two consultants, working within 'hard' medical science, differed on my category of risk. It is therefore not surprising that social workers and others will often experience challenges in making appropriate judgements. At certain points I was unsure whether Simon was moving towards, if not already into, the high-risk category. At other times in my career I also experienced difficulties towards the other end of the continuum. In fact, although not large in number, my encounters with situations in which a perceived risk was responded to in an excessive way outnumbered those where serious risk was missed. I believe the example below may have been a case of overreaction.

Example 10 Nadia and an overreaction to risk

Following a teacher reporting bruises and marks on the the legs of one of Nadia's teenage daughters, concerns were raise in relation to Nadia's parenting. When it became clear that Nadia was using a leather belt to physically chastise her child, a strong response included encouraging her daughter to proceed with criminal charges. This also ended Nadia's social care job with older people, since she was considered to be a potential danger to those for whom she was caring.

In my subsequent conversations with Nadia, who had been born in Africa, it became clearer that there were 'cultural' issues in relation to her parenting and use of physical chastisements rather than a propensity towards violence. She was open to modifying her approach in light of discussion about this. Although well intentioned and aimed to protect and safeguard the young person, I felt the response was excessive, and in effect caused significant unnecessary hardship, distress and difficulties within the family, depriving Nadia of a job she valued as well as being an important source of income for the family

There are continuing moves towards bringing a much wider range of violent actions, particularly within the parenting role, into the sphere of the criminal justice system in some jurisdictions. These endeavours are understandable in that more positive choices and non-violent behaviour may result from strong messages coming from the social care and criminal justice system (Walby et al. 2017). Positive parenting and relationships should be continually promoted. However, my personal default has always been more towards education and mediation rather than punishment and force. Returning once again to my prostate cancer analogy, a major study concluded that the potential mortality or quality-of-life benefits have at times been at the expense of harms from over-detection and over-treatment.[2] I think there are some lessons to be taken from this in responding to violence. There will be situations in which there is no evidence of a sustained campaign of coercive control, and it is reasonable to see the risk of future violence from a person as low. Of course, this can be a difficult position to adopt. However, by not doing so, there may be a danger that overly excessive interventions will impact harshly upon those, like Nadia (and Sarah), whose social circumstances may already be difficult. Ultimately, I believe that the law can only go so far in relation to the complexity of violence.

Working with uncertainty

At the risk of repetition, even when I had gathered significant amounts of information and knowledge about each person's situation (as described above), there was a degree of uncertainty. In other situations there will be more uncertainty, given that there will be minimal information available to help inform the response. This was the situation with regard to Amir, whose circumstances were described in Example 1 (The Letter, pp. 12–13). His example captures some of the challenges in assessing and having to make defensible decisions about risk within situations about which there is little knowledge or previous involvement.

Example 11 Amir and the risk of future violence

Amir's offence (referred to in Example 1) occurred during one of his partner Jane's regular visits, when she travelled from Northern Ireland with their young child to see him. She was upset to discover that Amir arrived to meet her and their child at the station in an intoxicated condition. She was angry and immediately started to berate him for his selfish behaviour. She was of a mind to call off her visit to him and return home with the baby.

Amir was irate at being scolded by Jane and he spoke to her in a threatening way, frightening her. He then forcibly grabbed the child from Jane, yelling threats at her and attempted to leave with the child in his arms. Fortunately, before he got very far, police were on the scene, and Amir was arrested and taken into custody. Jane, shocked and distressed, returned to Northern Ireland with their child. Following a period on remand, Amir received a prison sentence. He subsequently wrote to Jane from prison expressing his remorse and regret at his behaviour and asked her to consider continuing with their relationship. As indicated in Example 1, shortly after his release from prison, Jane agreed to a reconciliation, and sometime later they decided that Amir should come to Northern Ireland and they would live together as a family.

It was on the basis of the above information being shared with Social Services that Amir was asked to leave the family home until an assessment of the situation could be completed. However, apart from the above concerning act of reckless violence, nothing else was known about Amir as a person, nor his history. Similarly, there had never been any contact with Jane and her family. Nevertheless, decisions still had to be taken in relation to Amir's future role in Jane's and their child's life and the seriousness of the risks of living together as a family.

Being risk averse

Given Amir's offence, there was a reasonable argument to view him as an unacceptable risk and to make decisions accordingly. The 'best predictor of future behaviour is past behaviour' mantra, which had been reinforced in me as a Probation Officer, continues to be consistent with many studies (Hemphill et al. 2009). Such an approach appeared to be vindicated by other concerns that arose in the early stages of the assessment. These included Amir's explanation of his actions as being purely the result of his intoxicated condition. One of the social workers also noted that she felt from Amir's tone of voice that there was an 'arrogance' about him. She viewed his 'remorse' as being more akin to manipulation. She felt, at times that he tended to be psychologically and emotionally controlling towards Jane. She gave examples of hearing him pressurising Jane for money (as mentioned in Example 1, Amir had as yet no legal status in Northern Ireland and was struggling with living on £10 per week). Jane's parents also felt that Amir could manipulate Jane and that she was infatuated by someone who was older than her.

Risk and resource

Was there a danger that the above early observations reflected a mind-set that had, perhaps prematurely, classified Amir as dangerous and that was the end of it? (As he himself remarked to me in Example 1, this was what he sensed from some of those working with him.) The concerns were real and had to be taken into account. However, was the complex reality that he could be both a risk, but also a positive resource, being lost sight of? Dichotomous or 'either/or' thinking can lose sight of the complexity of risk (Day et al. 2009).

As the intervention progressed, Amir's commitment to his child became clear. The social worker who observed his contact visits commented on his attention and sensitivity, particularly in how he encouraged his child to read. Amir also shared a tragic personal story of fleeing civil war and the loss and break-up of his family. He was also prepared to engage in conversations about his violent behaviour. He acknowledged his recklessness and dangerousness in putting Jane and his young baby at risk. He also expressed some empathy for the distress he had caused both of them. He accepted that it would be reasonable for Jane to feel unsafe with and have fear of him. He expressed remorse and said he could now see that while alcohol was a factor, his actions also said something about a sense of entitlement and control which he was demanding to have over Jane. He maintained that his period of imprisonment was justified and had a salutary impact. Jane herself asserted that she did not feel controlled by Amir, and argued that, although her parents loved their grandchild, they did not fully accept Amir's cultural background.

Risk-aware practice and decision-making

In short, then, assessing and managing Amir's risk was dynamic and complex with conflicting messages emerging. Over a period of three months, each of the team had to try to make sense of their contacts and communication with Amir, Jane, her parents and the child. In dealing with Amir's use of violence, risk always had to be kept in mind. The accountability to the experiences and needs of Jane and her child in seeking to protect them from future harm was paramount (Jenkins 2009).

Ultimately, judgements about each party's attitudes and motivation and the potential for future violence had to be made (Parrott and Maguinness 2017). Intuition and gut feeling were important, but it also needed to be recognised that these could be wrong. Differing perspectives were analysed within a culture of challenge and circumspection (Ruch 2012). As it turned out, various pressures took their toll on Jane and Amir's relationship, which subsequently ended. However, the work done contributed to a less fraught process in which they were able to agree arrangements for Amir's future contact with his child.

Taking forward the conversations and risk

The conversations outlined in Part II of this volume are aimed at helping a person begin to both address and move towards non-violence within their life. These were also part of the engagement with Amir. They allowed judgements to be made across a range of areas, including his motivation, level of understanding, openness, empathy and commitment to safety. I had also engaged, to varying degrees, in these conversations with Peter, James, Sarah, Nadia and many others in different practice settings and going across the continuum of risk. They offer the possibility for safe and meaningful social work dialogue with the person who is using violence. As with Amir, they need to take place within, and also contribute to, the overarching and ongoing assessment and management of the continuing risks of further violence that a person may pose. As described in Chapter 5, they have the potential to provide a significant positive intervention in themselves, or, in situations of greater risk, they can provide an opening into other more specific or intense interventions. Of course, in situations of extreme violence, or where it may be associated with a serious mental health or intellectual difficulty, or where there may be concerns around sexual offending, more specialised and intrusive interventions will be required.

Conclusion

Some of the social workers involved in the tragic case referred to in Example 9 at the start of this chapter were subjected to death threats. I have also been part of a team and organisation experiencing savage media and public reactions in relation to a situation in which risks were not fully recognised or responded to and serious harm ensued. Some of the judgements were deserved; others were harsh and unfair. It is not surprising that there is a continuing preoccupation with risk. The practice with Nadia and some of the initially aversive reactions to Amir described above may be better understood within this context.

There will always be great challenges in appropriately assessing and managing risk without becoming overwhelmed or driven by our worse fears (Munroe 2011). Fear can be a helpful emotion at times, but it needs to be accompanied by clear and critical thinking. The importance of seeking meaningful engagement with the person who is using the violence should always be given serious consideration. This should be part of the overall assessment of the situation (Parrott and Maguinness 2017). The conversations presented in Part II of this volume are offered in support of this engagement.

Notes

1 I wrote down these words from Mayo Angelou which I heard on a long-forgotten television programme and they have stayed with me.
2 *Screening for Prostate Cancer* (Review). The Cochrane Library 2013. This Cancer Research UK study concluded that out of every 1000 men screened no lives would be saved but 20 men may be diagnosed with cancers unlikely to cause them any harm. This group may also have been put through unnecessary treatment, worry and potential complications such as infections, sexual dysfunction, and bladder and bowel control problems.

References

Barlow, J., Fisher, J.D. and Jones, D. (2012) *Systematic Review of Models of Analysing Significant Harm*. Department of Education, Research Report 199.

Campbell, B. (1993) *Goliath: Britain's Dangerous Places*. London: Methuen.

Day, A., Chung, D., O'Leary, P. and Carson, E. (2009) Programs for Men who Perpetrate Domestic Violence: An Examination of the Issues Underlying the Effectiveness of Intervention Programs. Family Violence, 24: 203–212.

Devaney, J. (2014) Male Perpetrators of Domestic Violence: How Should We Hold Them to Account. *The Political Quarterly*, 85(4): 480–486.

Dutton, D. (1998) *The Abusive Personality: Violence and Control in Intimate Relationships*. London: The Guilford Press.

Esbensen, F., Peterson, D., Taylor, T.J. and Freng, A. (2009) Similarities and Differences in Risk Factors for Violent Offending and Gang Membership. *The Australian and New Zealand Journal of Criminology*, 42(3): 310–335.

Hemphill, S.A., Smith, R., Toumbourou, J.W., Herrenkohl, T.I., Catalano, R.F., McMorris, B.J. and Romaniuk, H. (2009) Determinants of Youth Violence. *Australian and New Zealand Journal of Criminology*: 289–309.

Jenkins, A. (2009) *Becoming Ethical: A Parallel Journey with Men Who Have Abused*. Lyme Regis: Russell House Publishing.

Jones, A.S., Heckert, A., Zhang, Q. and Edward, H. (2010) Complex Behavioural Patterns and Trajectories of Domestic Violence Offenders. *Violence and Victims*, 25(1): 3–17.

Jones, D.W. (2008) *Understanding Criminal Behaviour: Psychosocial Approaches to Criminality*. Cullompton: Willan.

Kelly, L. and Westmarland, N. (2015) *Domestic Violence Perpetrator Programmes. Steps towards Change. Mirabal Final Report*. London and Durham: London Metropolitan University and Durham University.

Mariani, E., Özcan, B. and Goisis, A. (2017) Family Trajectories and Well-being of Children Born to Lone Mothers in the UK. *European Journal of Population*: 185–215.

Masson, H. (2004) Young Sex Offenders. In Kemshall, H. and Mc Ivor, G., *Managing Sex Offender Risk*. London: Jessica Kingsley.

Mathews, S., Jewkes, R. and Abrahams, N. (2011) 'I Had a Hard Life': Exploring Childhood Adversity in the Shaping of Masculinities among Men Who Killed an Intimate Partner in South Africa. *British Journal of Criminology*, 51: 960–977.

Mews, A., Di Bella, L. and Purver, M. (2017) Impact Evaluation of the Prison-based Core Sex Offender Treatment Programme. Ministry of Justice UK Analytical Series.

Milner, J. and Myers, S. (2016) *Working with Violence and Confrontation Using Solution Focused Approaches*. London: Jessica Kingsley.

Moffitt, T. (1993) 'Adolescence-limited and Life Course Persistent Antisocial Behaviour: A Developmental Taxonomy'. *Psychological Review*, 100(4): 674–701.

Munroe, E. (2011) *The Munroe Review of Child Protection – Final Report – A Child Centred System*. London: The Stationery Office.

Parrott, L. and Maguinness, N. (2017) *Social Work in Context. Theory and Concepts*. London: Sage.

Pinker, S. (2012) *The Better Angels of Our Nature*. London: Penguin.

Ruch, G. (2012) Two Halves Make a Whole: Developing Integrated Critical, Analytical and Reflective Thinking in Social Work Practice and Education. In Lishmen, J. (ed.), *Social Work Education and Training*. London: Jessica Kingsley.
Serin, R.C. and Preston, D.L. (2001) Managing and Treating Violent Offenders. In Ashford, J.B., Sales, B.D. and Reid, W. (eds), *Treating Adult and Juvenile Offenders with Special Needs*. Washington, DC: American Psychological Association.
Travers, O. (1999) *Behind the Silhouettes: Exploring the Myths of Child Sexual Abuse*. Belfast: Blackstaff Press.
Walby, S., Towers, J., Balderston, S., Corradi, C., Francis, B., Heiskanen, M., Helweg-Larsen, K., Mergaert, L., Olive, P., Palmer, E., Stöckl, H. and Strid, S (2017) *The Concept and Measurement of Violence*. Bristol: Policy Press.

Part II

Promoting non-violence

The eight conversations and the wall

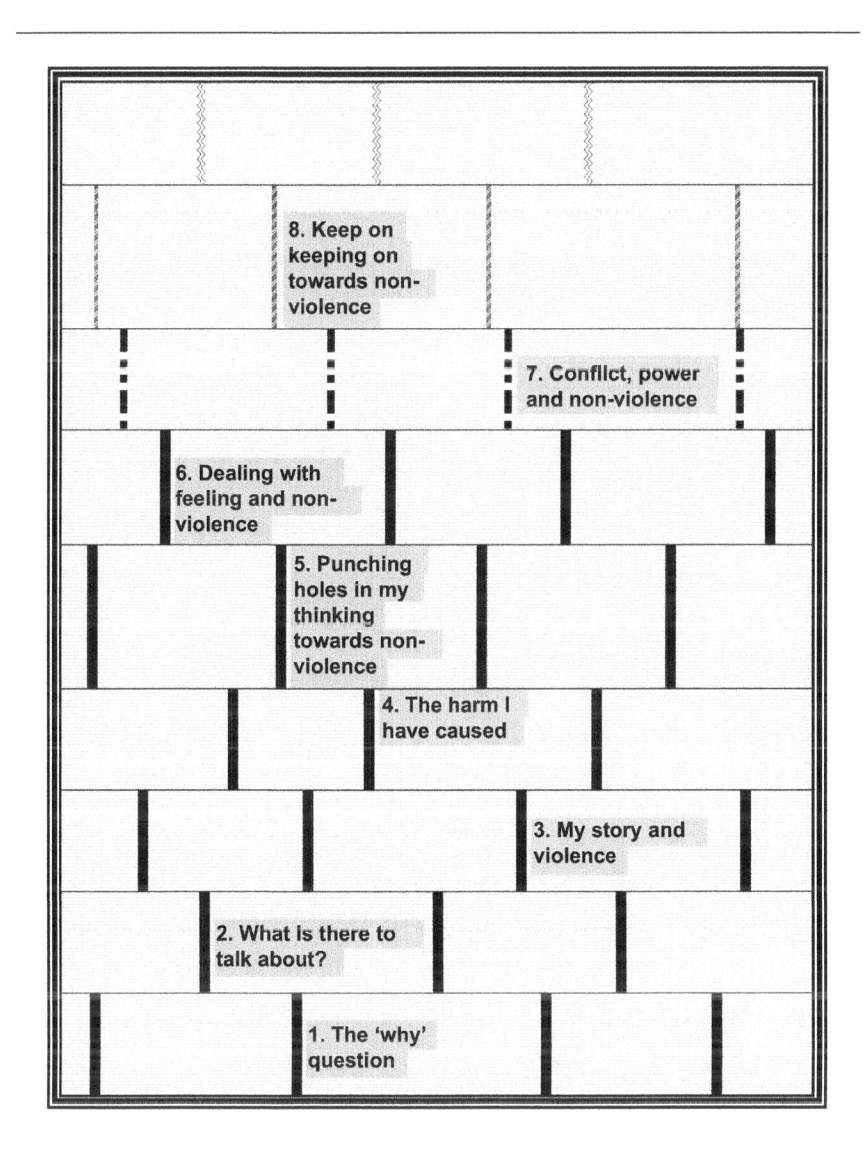

8. Keep on keeping on towards non-violence

7. Conflict, power and non-violence

6. Dealing with feeling and non-violence

5. Punching holes in my thinking towards non-violence

4. The harm I have caused

3. My story and violence

2. What is there to talk about?

1. The 'why' question

Chapter 5

Dialogue and the conversations

The eight conversations

Part I provided the foundation for the eight conversations which will now be presented. The conversations provide guidance for dialogue between the social worker and the person who is using violence. The Latin root of the word 'conversation' comes from the idea of conversion and change. The guidance on each of the conversations recognises this and also the reality that 'each utterance deepens, maintains, or distances the relationship between those in the conversation' (Garrido 2016, p. 117).

Reflecting the essence of person-centred social work, the conversations also recognise the reality that positive change towards safety and non-violence cannot be forced on someone or achieved by some sort of manipulation. If it is going to happen, change needs to come from the individual.

Each of the conversations also connects to a key message from the Northern Ireland Peace Process. This linkage is briefly outlined in the introductory page for each conversation. Whether or not it is helpful to share this is at the discretion of the worker.

As already indicated in the introduction, the material in each of the conversations may be used flexibly.

Promoting non-violence (PNV)

The option to work through all eight face-to-face conversations sequentially to create a more structured intervention may be considered. The guidance that follows reflects this approach.

At the outset, the informed consent of the person is required. The person will also need to agree and commit to actively thinking about, reflecting on and reporting back on the issue of violence within her or his life between face-to-face contacts. Element 2 in the first conversation sets out guidance on agreeing to work in such a way (see pp. 65–67).

How the conversations are taken forward in terms of the duration and the make-up of each interaction may be negotiated with the person. Each of the eight conversations contains four core outcome-based elements, each of which should be worked through before moving on to the next. Upon completion of each element, the person's own conclusions may be summarised and recorded.

While it is possible to cover an entire conversation within one session, this does not have to be the case. As stated previously, there is always discretion, as, for example, with a young person who may prefer to engage with 'bite-sized' short interactions.

Check-ins

Begin each meeting (conversation) by allowing the person to share how things are, and then reflect on the issue of violence within their life since the previous meeting.

The check-in cannot be too tightly scripted or time limited. The goal is to support and encourage the person, mainly through open questions and reflections, to help them become more aware of their behaviour (see Figure 5.1).

Check-ins should seek to affirm those situations in which the person may have found ways to deal with a challenging scenario in a safer way than before. Even the slightest moves in this direction should be reinforced, and any positives, however small, reflected back. Exceptions to the use of violence

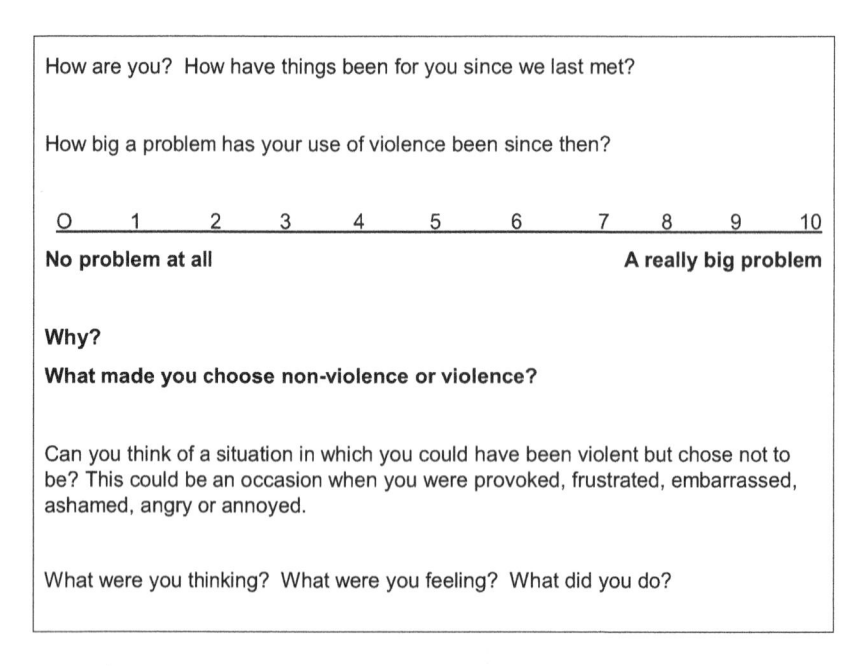

How are you? How have things been for you since we last met?

How big a problem has your use of violence been since then?

| 0 | 1 | 2 | 3 | 4 | 5 | 6 | 7 | 8 | 9 | 10 |

No problem at all   **A really big problem**

Why?
What made you choose non-violence or violence?

Can you think of a situation in which you could have been violent but chose not to be? This could be an occasion when you were provoked, frustrated, embarrassed, ashamed, angry or annoyed.

What were you thinking? What were you feeling? What did you do?

Figure 5.1 Possible check-In questions for use by the worker.

that are presented should be identified and affirmed. Ultimately, the aim of the conversations is to build up a recognition and confidence that the person does have control over their behaviour and the ability, even within challenging situations, to choose non-violent pathways.

It is important not to try to persuade or convince the person that they have handled a difficult situation well. The conversation should allow the person to evaluate their own actions and draw their own conclusions. The approach which applies throughout is akin to holding a mirror in front of the person and reflecting back what they are saying. This may sometimes help them to see a more accurate view of reality and different ways of dealing with challenging situations (Musson 2017).

However, in using the motivational interviewing approach, the skill is reflecting back the right issues. Clear positive statements about trying to change should be affirmed and re-enforced. Statements that are ambivalent or that try to justify questionable actions or appear to go against the person's stated goals should also be reflected back in a non-judgemental way. This may push the person a little deeper and create some internal discomfort within their thinking.

Bringing down the wall: outcomes, checking out and closure

If the beginning of each session or conversation is important then so too is the ending. This applies to one-off, opportunity-led interactions as well as sessions within a more structured programmed approach.

The final element involves recapping and agreeing, in simple language, a short summary of what has taken place. This should include any significant violence-related matter from the check-in. In addition, the person's conclusions and learning from each of the subsequent elements may be summarised and recorded.

Each session should move to a close with an expression of appreciation to the person for his or her efforts and commitment to bringing down the wall blocking the path to non-violence. Following a reminder to keep doing their personal daily reflection on violence, and a clear statement that the 'work' is finished, the session then closes with the person's response, in a word or two, to the following two questions:

1. Mention one thing from our conversation today that you will think more about.
2. How are you feeling as you leave?

(Of course, any concerns about the person's emotional state should be responded to.)

The core elements

The check-in and closure are the book-end elements for each individual session. The guidance for these has been provided above, rather than repeating it in each conversation. Between the check-in and the closure, there may be up to four core elements that may be worked through. There is discretion in how this is done. The elements break down the challenge of helping the person move to non-violence into achievable tasks; to focus on goal-limited objectives rather than on a seemingly impenetrable violence problem (Novaco and Chemtob 1998). Hammer's (2006, p. 11) assertion that 'work done without creativity is simply brutality' should be borne in mind in working to help people with change. An over-reliance on dry didactic information giving should be avoided.

There is also a danger of escalating oneself to the role of an expert within the conversations which needs to be avoided (Turnell and Edwards 1999). Of course, there is an important educational element within the conversations and some information will have to be presented. This should be done within a spirit of self-directed adult learning in which the person decides what to take and what to leave. In other words, it is about encouraging the person to frame their own learning needs, to reflect on the presented material to do with violence as it fits to their own circumstances and to begin to draw their own conclusions as to how they need to try things out or go forward. It involves the idea of a continuous cycle of learning and reflection within a safe and supported context (Kolb 2015).

The key is to provide creative opportunities to allow the person to put their thoughts and feelings into words (and/or on paper for those who like to write) to make them more real and concrete, to slow things down, so that they can be elaborated and reflected on in some depth. I often use a large flip chart spread out on the table, and key points can be noted or represented in various ways. The large sheet can also be useful when working with an interpreter, who can write out key words or points in the person's own language. Each element ends when the person has demonstrated and confirmed its expected outcomes in terms of their own conclusions. (As stated previously, these should be briefly recorded before moving on to the next element.)

Conclusion

The conversations provide choice in terms of the nature and intensity of the approach taken. Everything is negotiable, and, as stressed in Part I of this volume, the goal is to work in partnership and to co-produce something that actually may impact positively in helping someone move to non-violence and greater safety in life.

In whatever way the conversations are taken forward, it is critical to hold on to the reality that asking a person to talk about her or his use of violence will be difficult, and 'that acknowledging a compromising truth about ourselves is among our most painful experiences' (Pinker 2012, p. 593). All the conversations need to occur within a relationship of sensitivity and compassion.

As with many areas of face-to-face social work practice, there will, at times, be tension in balancing the necessity of being supportive and responsive to the person while striving to maintain a structure, shape and focus to the conversation.

The guidance that follows will not be offered in the third person. It will speak directly to 'you' the worker. Similarly, the Resources contained in Appendix 1 will be in the first person, 'I', to allow the person to take ownership. These are referred to throughout the conversations and may be used to develop particular issues and to help the person with his or her personal journey of change.

Finally, the guidance is written to meet those circumstances in which the worker and the person doing the work are new to each other. Of course, if this is happening within the context of an already well-established positive professional relationship, then, as appropriate, a lighter touch can be taken with the material.

References

Garrido, A. (2016) *Redeeming Conflict: 12 Habits for Christian Leaders.* Notre Dame: Ave Maria Press.

Hammer, M. (2006) *The Barefoot Helper: Mindfulness and Creativity in Social Work and the Helping Professions.* Lyme Regis: Russell House Publishing.

Kolb, D.A. (2015) *Experiential Learning: Experiences as the Source of Learning and Development.* New Jersey: Pearson Education Inc.

Musson, P. (2017) *Making Sense of Theory and its Application to Social Work Practice.* St Albans: Critical Publishing.

Novaco, R.W. and Chemtob, C.M. (1998) Anger and Trauma: Conceptualisation, Assessment and Treatment. In Follette, V.M., Ruzek, J.I. and Abueg, F.R. (eds), *Cognitive Behavioural Therapies for Trauma.* London: The Guilford Press.

Pinker, S. (2012) *The Better Angels of Our Nature.* London: Penguin.

Turnell, A. and Edwards, S. (1999) *Signs of Safety: A Solution and Safety Oriented Approach to Child Protection.* London: W.W. Norton.

Chapter 6

Conversation 1
The 'why' question

A famous television advertisement, made in 1992 asked the key question about the Northern Ireland conflict: Why continue to suffer it?[1] At the time, the peace process referred to in the introduction was in its early stages. It was, as it continues to be, torturous and slow. Many of those previously committed to violence took years in considering this question before finding their own reasons as to 'why' they should take a path to non-violence. Working towards peace only appeared to make progress with those 'who genuinely wanted to move on'.[2] At the time of writing, the twentieth anniversary of the Good Friday (Belfast) Agreement, there are still a small number of people who continue to use violence in pursuit of their goals. All efforts to persuade, cajole and to promote non-violence have been resisted. The 'peace' walls are still needed and still standing.

Similarly, and as indicated in Chapter 3, motivation is a crucial issue with a person who has been using common violence within some aspect of his or her life. There may be a 'wall' blocking the path to non-violence. Like Belfast's peace walls, and the one shown in the introduction, the person's wall will only come down if (s)he really wants it to. The first conversation addresses this issue and 'why' the person wants to move away from violence. What are the person's reasons for doing so? These are explored within the positive goals that the person has for their own future and meeting their positive primary needs that all human beings seek.

There is no point in going forward with the work unless the person has their own answer to the 'why' question. The answer: a desire not to continue to suffer it in terms of the harm their violence is doing to others and to themselves.

Thought bubbles:

- I need to know what I am getting into
- Being non-violent fits with the most important goals in my life
- My life balance needs to be right to help me change
- Change needs to be important to me and something I can do
- Change is ongoing and never finished
- There is a difference in moving from what I don't want to moving towards what I do want (Coyle 2013)

The 'why' question: key messages

Being clear about why I want to do this work will help bring the wall down.

CONTENT/OBJECTIVES

1. Welcome and check-in
2. What's the deal: agreeing to have the conversations
3. My motivation: why I want to do this
4. Choosing non-violence: where am I in making the change?
5. How do my important goals and life balance fit with non-violence?
6. Bringing down the wall: outcomes, check-out and closure

Element 1 Welcome and check-in

The invitation to work towards non-violence and safety is the starting point for the first conversation in promoting non-violence (PNV). Give a warm welcome and affirm the fact that the person has agreed to at least think about the invitation.

Outline the content of the conversation above. The key messages may also be shared, verbally, on flip chart, on power point or around the room.

Give a personal introduction if you are working with someone new.

Make clear that the conversations are about supporting and working alongside the person and the overall purpose is for the person to:

- gain a greater understanding of their use of violence and its effects;
- learn about and practise ways to be non-violent;
- choose non-violence in their behaviour within relationships, family and community.

Reassure the person that everyone has some difficulties with issues around aggression, violence and anger. A 'safe' personal example of being aggressive within a relationship, family or community context could be shared to reinforce this key point.

Before moving on, ask the person why he or she is here – what is their understanding of what they are undertaking? This may be more of an issue if it is your first meeting, and should not be rushed. Even though the ultimate goal is to encourage change, it is always better to start with the person rather than with the issue. The person should be given all the time he or she needs to answer the question, and ultimately it is their decision if they wish to move forward.

If the person appears resistant or ambivalent about going forward, the following relatively safe and straightforward exercise may be used at this point. However, if the person is clearly motivated and is acknowledging a serious problem with their use of violence, the exercise could be deferred to the next element.

Place two chairs a short distance apart from each other. Agree that one of the chairs represents how the person currently feels about their use of violence. To begin, focus on this first chair. Make it clear that it does not have to be analysed any further or judged, other than that it represents the person's own perception of where they are in relation to the use of violence at this point in their life. Emphasise that for now, the person should not mention any specific details about any aspect of their use of violence. It is just about their general feelings about the use of violence in their life.

Explain that the other chair represents the person's ideal position in terms of their use of violence not being a problem in their life and how they would like things to be for them. Ask the question: Does there need to be a second chair? If the person is happy sitting in the first chair, they are indicating to you that they do not currently have any problem with the issue of the use of violence in their life. There is absolutely no reason or need to try to change anything about their behaviour. There is probably no point in continuing with the conversation if this is the case.

If the person chooses to sit in the second chair, this is showing a recognition of not being content with current behaviour and a need to try to get to a new place. This should be affirmed. Ask the person to also imagine that there is a wall between the two chairs. Ask how big and how thick the wall is. How easy or hard will it be to knock this wall down? Where is the wall at its strongest or thickest – in a relationship, at home, somewhere else? Where is the violence mostly happening?

The key question is whether the person wants or feels it will be worthwhile to try to bring this wall down that may be blocking their path to a non-violent, safer and more settled life. It may be appropriate to acknowledge that the person may already be on their way to the 'second chair' and have been working to get safer themselves. Hopefully, this work will reinforce and enhance their efforts.

This conversation may move on when the introductions have been completed and both you and the person have shared and recorded your understanding of why you are here and the person has indicated a need and a desire to work towards positive change and non-violence.

Element 2 What's the deal: agreeing to have the conversations

In the second element you will make the explicit offer to the person to engage in a series of conversations aimed at helping and encouraging them to move away from common violence towards safety. The nature of the conversations the person will be getting into should be made clear. Specifically, they will be guided by four underpinning values which largely mirror the social work values outlined in Chapter 3. If you are already in a social work relationship with the person, then much of what follows will have already been made clear and a lighter touch can be used in going forward into the conversations. The detailed guidance is intended for those situations where you and the person are in a new professional relationship.

i. *Respect.* You should emphasise that the conversations will not involve negative judgements, put-downs or attempts to trap the person. You can demonstrate respect right from the outset and agree to meet at times and places that best suit the person, and that you will be punctual.[3]

Respect should be extended to any other parties who may be referred to, but are not in the conversation, particularly if they have been on the receiving end of the person's violence.

The conversations may only continue within a context of mutual respect.

ii. *Safety*. Advise the person, that the conversations will go forward following their undertaking to do their best to refrain from any form of serious physical, sexual or other violence during the period they are taking place. Of course, and returning to the broad definition of violence presented in Chapter 2, it would be unrealistic to expect someone to desist from all the controlling aspects of their behaviour that could be deemed violent. Hopefully, doing this work may help increase awareness of the damaging effects of more subtle forms of coercive behaviour.

However, the avoidance of clearly illegal physical force or threatening actions, as we saw with Simon in Chapter 3 (p. 36) is paramount.

Furthermore, and if appropriate, the person must be aware that by doing this work they may also be agreeing to you contacting those who have been on the receiving end of the person's violence. (More detail is provided on this in Appendix 2, p. 153).

Reassure the person that the conversations themselves will be 'safe'. They are not intended to cause upset nor distress. Again, as discussed in Chapter 3, sensitivity to mental health or trauma-related issues needs to be demonstrated throughout the conversations.

Point out that sometimes a person may feel a little 'shook up' or challenged or possibly ashamed about aspects of their behaviour – these can be positive signs. In the unlikely event that the person becomes distressed, an offer of support will be given. Point out that there is always the right to opt out of a particular exercise that may be too distressful or upsetting without having to give reasons. The message should be that the conversations may be challenging at times but are ultimately about learning, growth and positive personal development.

iii. *Participation*. The conversations will be active, face-to-face two-way encounters. Stress that you are not an 'expert' who will be telling the person how to think, feel or behave. Neither does the person have to agree with everything you say. Violence is a complex issue and you can learn from each other. It's about actively engaging with the work, listening to each other's views, reflecting on this, and you and the person reaching their conclusions.

However, the person does need to agree to your request to think about and reflect on violence-related issues both during and between meetings and conversations. There is a requirement that the person takes a few minutes at the end of each day to think about and reflect on that day's experiences with violence or its avoidance. Encourage the person to keep a short written daily note of some of their experiences and reflections. These mental or written recollections will become part of the opening check-in at each subsequent meeting. You can give the person a copy of PNV Resource 1 (Appendix 1) to take away, or a small notebook.

(Further guidance on the check-in is provided in Chapter 5, pp. 58–89).

iv. *Effectiveness*. Point out that the conversations reflect the latest ideas on what can be helpful to a person with change. Everything will be geared towards encouraging and supporting the person to take ownership of the issue of violence in their life and work towards being non-violent. Ultimately, the eventual outcome will depend on the person. They need to be ready, willing and able to face this challenge. If it is something that is really important to the person, (s)he will find the time and make the commitment to it. If the person does not do this, then despite what they say, it may be that the issue is of no real consequence to them and the dialogue is unlikely to be effective. Effective engagement and commitment may also not be possible if the person is experiencing significant mental health or addiction problems.

Confidentiality and consent issues may have already been clarified prior to the agreement to embark on these conversations. If needs be, these can be made clear again. In relation to confidentiality, the bottom line is that this cannot be guaranteed if the person's safety, or that of another person, is at risk. Furthermore, if the person provides specific and detailed information in relation to a serious criminal offence having being committed, then in many jurisdictions you will not be able to keep this confidential.[4]

In addition, the person needs to give informed consent to involvement in such work, particularly if it forms part of an overall agreed intervention to address the use of violence within their relationships, family or community (as with Amir in Chapter 4, pp. 49–51). As such, you may have to record and share with others the person's attendance and level of participation. However, the 'records' of sessions will primarily be summaries of the person's own conclusions in terms of the outcomes of each conversation. Most of what is said in the conversations will stay there.

This conversation may move on when the person has given their permission and agreement to commit to work with you in terms of the process, respective responsibilities and the underpinning values.

Element 3 My motivation: why I want to do this

The conversation can now return to its core, and that is the 'why' question. What is the person's own answer as to why he or she thinks or feels that they need to do something about the use of violent behaviour in their lives and to become safer? In other words, it is about clarifying the person's own perspectives on the use of violence and just how big an issue it is for them (Ruch 2013).

There may well be various external forces and circumstances operating in the person's life that are encouraging him or her to think about making some changes and these can be part of your discussion. Indeed, sometimes a crisis moment (for example, in the situation where restrictions are imposed upon contact with children) may lead to a greater willingness to seek or accept help (Brooks et al. 2014). The essence of this element is to invite the person, in their own words, to reflect on why he or she wants to make any efforts to change their behaviour, primarily in relation to the use of violence. In other words, what is their internal motivation? The question for the person to consider is: 'Why do I want to bring the wall down?'

PNV Resource 2, which references the two chairs metaphor and the wall, may also be used. It contains two scaling questions that can allow deeper exploration of the person's perspective: first, how important is dealing with their use of violence in their life; second, how confident are they that they can bring down the wall and get to safety.

This conversation may move on when the person has self-assessed the importance of the issue of staying safer in their lives and also their confidence in working towards such an outcome, as well as identifying some of the blocks that may get in the way.

Element 4 Choosing non-violence: where am I in making the change?

Return to the wall that has to come down and gently explore where the person is in doing this and making a long-lasting change towards non-violence and safety. Introduce the well-known cycle of change model that can be used to show the challenges involved in making change (Prochaska et al. 1992).

I have found that the model is more helpful if it is first illustrated in relation to a separate 'safer' aspect of human behaviour such as diet, smoking, alcohol use, gambling, keeping fit, etc. Agree on an example from the person's own experience or from someone they know where there has been a process of change. Use this example to illustrate a messy back-and-forth process of change (more guidance is provided for this in PNV Resource 3). The exercise can also be done more experientially within the room and using chairs to represent the various stages between which the person can physically move in bringing the ideas to life.

As indicated in PNV Resource 3, after processing the 'safe' example of change, the challenge for the person is to position themselves on the stages of change cycle, in relation to making change towards non-violence. The issue of the person having already tried and slipped back in their efforts to change can also be gently explored. Be positive in that slip-ups or relapses, which can be very discouraging at the time, may also be viewed as another step towards ultimately succeeding with the change (Howarth and Morrison 2001).

You may find some of the following questions helpful in further exploring with a person their own particular cycle of change:

- Becoming who I am has taken many years – how can I change all that now?
- How much do I need to understand to help me change?
- How much responsibility should I take for my need to change?
- How will challenging my thinking help me to change?
- If I slip back how can I pick myself up quickly?
- Why am I trying to change – is it for myself or for others?

This conversation may move on when the person has explored some of the challenges involved in building towards long-term change and has self-assessed where they are on the cycle of change towards non-violence and safer behaviour.

Element 5 How do my important goals and life balance fit with non-violence?

The penultimate element is broken into two closely related parts. First, ask the person to identify and reflect on important goals they currently have for their future lives (see PNV Resource 4). An open question asking where they would like to be in three years' time may bring these goals to the surface. Ultimately, the hope is that the person can connect being safer to some higher purpose in their life (Kerr 2013). Of course, if one of the key personal goals is becoming non-violent you should affirm this. In the spirit of motivational interviewing, you should recognise and further encourage the person's energy in working towards a goal that comes from a positive response to the 'why' question. There is strength in, rather than moving from something undesirable, seeing change more as moving towards something that is wanted (Coyle 2013).

Gently explore other identified goals, particularly in terms of how these may be impacted upon by the use of violence. It may be possible to probe further what the person's goals say about their values and beliefs in life and where they want to get to. Again, this may allow you to place the abusive and violent behaviour that the person is trying to move away from within the context of his or her own ethical preferences and strivings (Jenkins 2009).

The importance of the person's goals should never be minimised. Pro-social goals can then become your driving force. You should never lose sight of these during every element within all future conversations in your efforts to continue to support the goals that the person has identified. Even with a younger person, the development of clear, self-set, achievable goals can be helpful in addressing the slide towards delinquency, including violence (Caroll et al. 2013).

Of course, the achievement of life goals may well depend to a significant degree on life balance (Covey 2004). The already mentioned PNV Resource

4 also presents a simple model in this regard. It contains trigger questions you can use to explore and record issues in relation to how the person is physically, mentally and emotionally, and the interrelationships between these. For example, when I began working with Amir (see pp. 12–13 and 49–50), he did not have legal residence status and was not allowed to work. He did not have enough income to eat properly. My work began with him in June and he joked that it was just as well it was Ramadan! I tried to help him with accessing charities but his life situation remained difficult.

Some of the issues identified within this exercise have already been flagged up in Chapter 3 in relation to the critical importance of a holistic assessment of the person's needs and circumstances. These should have been addressed prior to engaging in this intervention. You may need to review in terms of resources or supports that may be required. You should ensure that any work at change in relation to moving towards non-violence should never lose sight of the bigger picture of the individual's life and his or her overall well-being. As Maslow (1970) pointed out many years ago, individuals are unlikely to be able to focus in depth on personal work (in any area of their lives) if their survival, safety and more basic living requirements are not attended to first.

Returning to PNV Resource 4, invite the person to identify with the big circle going around the triangle. Make it clear that they do not have to – it's a matter of personal choice which will be respected. Point out that, for some, it may represent a religious belief system and something greater outside human life. In other words, the transcendent, the spiritual, something that guides and directs, and that gives an ultimate purpose for existence, that can be intimately linked to the person's health and life and ultimately to the belief that change is possible. If this is relevant to the person you should recognise this as important, particularly in valuing diversity and personalisation.

You can also acknowledge the growing body of study and research into mindfulness techniques, emotional intelligence, diet, exercise, and also various spiritual practices that may all contribute to greater life balance. Your overall message to the person is a simpler and common-sense one. Namely, in striking a healthy balance in taking care of themselves, the best formula is about all things in moderation (O'Leary 2016). If there are clear gaps or problems, then the person can be encouraged to think about, and if possible be supported in availing themselves of resources that may make necessary enhancements to their quality of life.

The conversation may move on when important life goals and life balance issues have been reflected on and the person has made some connection between these and their goal of non-violence. There should also be confirmation and agreement that the person is in a reasonable position to work towards meaningful change.

Element 6 Bringing down the wall: outcomes, check-out and closure

The guidance for this element is provided on p. 59.

Notes

1 The advertisement may be accessed on YouTube by entering 'The Cat's in the Cradle Advert N Ireland Troubles'.
2 This comment, reported in the *Irish News* on 17 November 2017 (a Belfast newspaper), was made by the chief executive of a consortium comprising members from various conflict resolution bodies and from both universities in Northern Ireland. Its establishment was agreed by the main political parties and by both the British and Irish governments in 2015 to encourage those still committed to violence to move towards peace.
3 I remember being disappointed on one occasion when a social work team refused to accommodate a man whose employment involved lengthy sea trips as a fisherman on a trawler boat requiring him to forgo significant earnings. Encouraging motivation is about removing as many blockages as possible rather than putting them in front of people.
4 For example, the 1967 Criminal Law Act (Norther Ireland) makes it an offence to fail to report to police that a potential crime has taken place.

References

Brooks, O., Burman, M., Lombard, N. Mc Ivor, G., Stevenson-Hastings, L. and Kyle, D. (2014) *Violence against Women: Effective Interventions and Practices with Perpetrators. A Literature Review.* Scottish Centre for Crime and Justice Research Report No. 05/2014.
Caroll, A., Gordon, K., Haynes, M. and Houghton, S. (2013) Goal Setting and Self-Efficacy Among Delinquent, at-Risk and Not At-Risk Adolescents. *Journal of Youth Adolescence*, 42: 431–443.
Covey, S. (2004) *The 8th Habit From Effectiveness to Greatness.* London. Simon & Schuster.
Coyle, D. (2013)*The Green Platform.* Wicklow: Ballpoint Press.
Howarth, J. and Morrison, T. (2001) Assessment of Parental Motivation to Change. In Howarth, J., *The Child's World.* London: Jessica Kingsley.
Jenkins, A. (2009) *Becoming Ethical: A Parallel, Political Journey with Men Who Have Abused.* Lyme Regis: Russell House Publishing.
Kerr, J. (2013) *Legacy.* London: Constable.
Maslow, A. (1970) *Motivation and Personality* (2nd edn). New York: Harper & Row.
O'Leary, D (2016) *The Happiness Habit.* Dublin: Columba Press.
Prochaska, J.O., Diclemente, C.C. and Norcross, J.C.(1992) In Search of How People Change: Applications to Addictive Behaviours. *American Psychologist*, 47(9): 1104 –1114.
Ruch, G. (2013) Understanding Contemporary Social Work: We Need to Talk More about Relationships. In Parker, J. and Doel, M., *Professional Social Work.* London: Learning Matters.

Chapter 7

Conversation 2
What is there to talk about?

The violence which disfigured Northern Ireland during its long conflict was extreme and multi-faceted. Its roots could be found in a long history of inequality, abuses of power and previous bitter conflicts. However, ultimately, various individuals and groupings decided to use violence in pursuit of their goals. Much of this violence was physical force but it was also accompanied by other manifestations, including intimidation, threats, and psychological and emotional abuse, all directed towards controlling the lives of others. Even today, years later, many of those who believed in such deeds have never talked about exactly what they did. By not acknowledging the violence that they have used they have not even begun to take responsibility for it nor to address the harm it caused. This has been and continues to be a running sore throughout the peace process.

The second conversation provides the person with the opportunity to bring forward the common violence that will need to be talked about. In doing this, the person needs to be clear about the wide-ranging nature of common violence and to begin to recognise the full range of their actions that may have been violent. Their actions, which are putting them on the wrong side of the wall, should also be related to the thinking and feeling that may go with them. Work to change has to be about hearts and minds as well as the actions. The conversation provides an opportunity for the person to be open about the extent of their use of violence and begin to get some understanding of this in bringing down the wall and committing to non-violence.

Conversation 2: What is there to talk about? 73

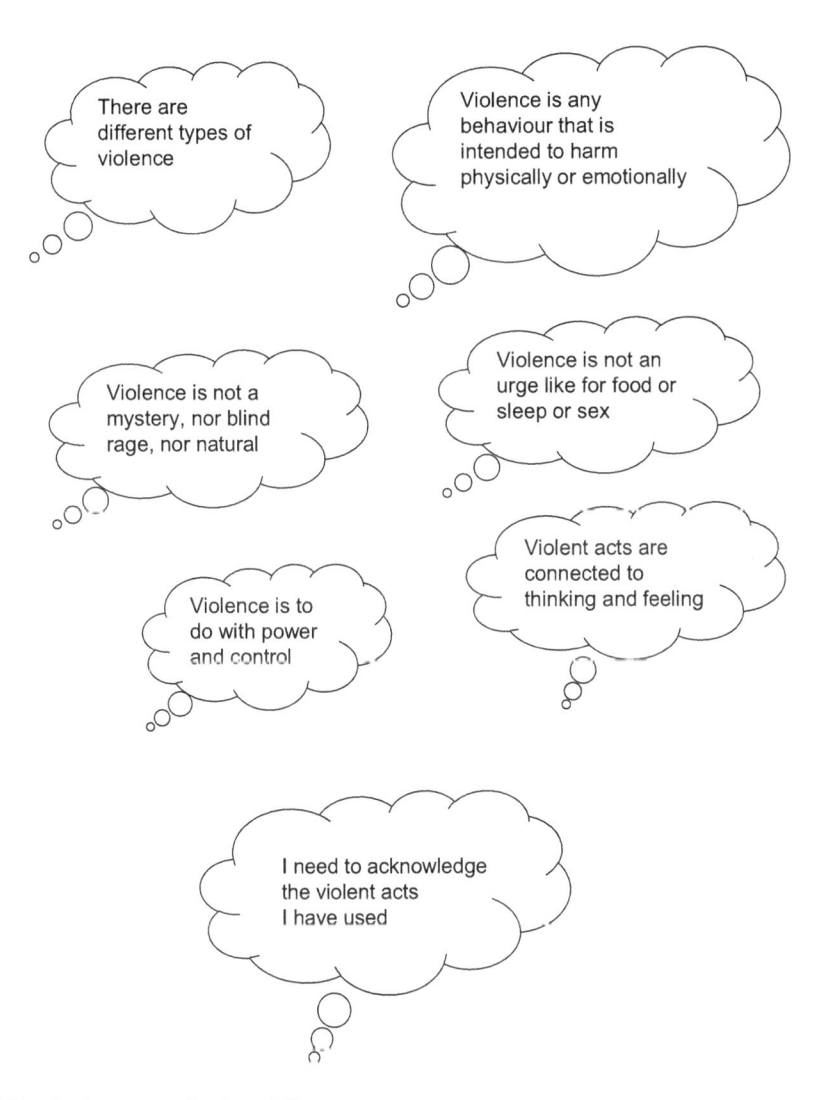

- There are different types of violence
- Violence is any behaviour that is intended to harm physically or emotionally
- Violence is not a mystery, nor blind rage, nor natural
- Violence is not an urge like for food or sleep or sex
- Violence is to do with power and control
- Violent acts are connected to thinking and feeling
- I need to acknowledge the violent acts I have used

What is there to talk about? Key messages

Acknowledging and trying to understand my violent acts will help bring the wall down.

CONTENT/OBJECTIVES

1. Welcome and check-in
2. Understanding what common violence is
3. My use of violence
4. Understanding violent behaviour as a mix of actions, thoughts and feelings
5. Linking my violent acts to my thinking and feelings
6. Bringing down the wall: outcomes, checking out and closure

Element 1 Welcome and check-in

Give a warm welcome to the person and, if following a more structured approach, begin with a reminder/summary of the person's agreed conclusions and learning outcomes from the previous meeting or full conversation.

At the start of this conversation, make the general point that we are living in a world beset with wars, conflicts and many manifestations of terrorism and politically inspired violence. However, the focus of this work is on the forms of more common violence that occurs within relationships, families and communities. The purpose of the conversation is to help the person be open about the extent and the ways in which they use violent acts, and how these may link to their thinking and feelings.

The key messages may be referred to before sharing the content above so that the person knows what will be discussed.

Referring to guidance on pp. 58–59 allow the person to check in.

Element 2 Understanding what common violence is

Ask the person to take a moment to think about and give their own definition of violence in no more than 12 words. Emphasise that there is no right or wrong answer, it's not a test and that you will share some of your thoughts with them so that there can be agreement on what is being talked about. The person can think out loud with their answers, or write them down on a sheet of paper or on the flip chart; it may be a list of words or a sentence – it's up to them. Whatever way you do it, keep it light and safe, and stop it at the point when 12 or so words have been reached.

You may have to work to agreed definitions within your agency and legal context, but your primary aim is to help the person see the breadth and depth of violence and its relationship to control; in other words, any behaviour that is intended to harm, physically or emotionally (WHO 2004). PNV Resource 5 (Appendix 1) which contains a definition may be used to make links between what is on the person's list and encouraging an appreciation (if it is not already there) of the breadth of violence. You can also use the same resource, which contains brief examples of violence to help widen the definition of violence that will be worked with. Try to help the person get a real sense of the different types of common violence:

1. Physical force
2. Threatening actions
3. Sexually abusive actions
4. Bossing and controlling
5. Emotional/psychological abuse.

Conversation 2: What is there to talk about? 75

Help the person identify at least five or so examples of each of the above types of violence.

Question 5 in the resource sheet will move the conversation on to the person's view as to how much of these various types of violence actually occur. Acknowledge that a lot of it is hidden and not reported. Since much of it also happens in private and behind 'closed doors', nobody really knows just how much violence occurs. The points below, which summarise the main outcomes from the mountain of research into the topic, reviewed in Chapter 2, may be used to inform the conversation:

- There are a lot of different types of violence within intimate relationships, families and communities – it is endemic.
- Violence goes across classes, races and cultures.
- There are particularly high levels of violence between young men, including gang violence, which is more prevalent in socially deprived areas.
- Violence remains a major public health issue for women and children in their relationships and families, most of it from men.
- Men and women can also be on the receiving end of such violence from women.

The conversation may move on when the person has demonstrated an understanding and acceptance of the wide-ranging nature of violence, its prevalence across society and that there is some sort of gender element within much of it.

Element 3 My use of violence

The person should now connect the general picture of violence explored above with their own personal situation. In particular, try to identify the range of violent actions the person has used in their relationships, family or community.

PNV Resource 6 provides further examples of various manifestations of the different types of violence referred to in the previous element. This may be used to assist the person to share and record the types of violence they may have used.

Emphasise that, at this stage, while the person needs to identify the actions they have used and to be as open and honest as they can, they do not need to give specific details in relation to any incidents of violence, particularly if they have not been adjudicated within the justice system. Neither is it the time for explanations or justifications. At this point it is just about which of the actions listed in Resource 6 have been used.

Again, you could refer to the wall in terms of how it will ever be knocked down if the person is not clear and open about the extent of their problem to start with. Accept the disclosure in a matter-of-fact way, without censure, disapproval, judgement or shock. While guilt or shame may be an issue for the person, the approach should not be about shaming and any significant disclosures should be affirmed as an important step towards safety.

You can also use Resource 6 to encourage the person to drill down further into the location, extent, intentionality and seriousness of the violent acts that have been used. Alternatively, different chairs or places in the room, or circles drawn on a flip chart could be used to represent each of the five areas to gently but thoroughly explore the various aspects of the person's use of violence.

The issue of how power is playing out in the person's use of violent actions should also be considered, as indicated in Resource 6.

Before concluding, the person's reactions and feelings from doing this difficult personal work should be explored.

The conversation may move on when the person has acknowledged a significant use of various violent actions in terms of their type, location, extent, pattern, seriousness and relationship with power issues.

Element 4 Understanding violent behaviour as a mix of actions, thoughts and feelings

Ask the person to now consider an example of an occurrence of violence and to analyse it. The example will not be about the person but about someone else's use of violence.

Whatever example is chosen, it must contain enough information within it that the observer can identify specific violent acts, as well as being able to get some sense of the violent person's thinking and emotional state leading up to the violence. Ask the person to listen to or watch and then to analyse the example of behaviour (short clips from YouTube, television programmes or films can provide useful examples; these do not need to be too graphic). Again, a light touch should be used. Emphasise that it is not a test. It is just a way into beginning to think about human behaviour and particularly the use of violence, which is complex.

Using PNV Resource 7, or three corners of the room, ask the person to try to identify the specific violent actions, thoughts and feelings relevant to the person who has been violent in the video or story. The actions should be straightforward enough. You may need to give more help in relation to the thinking and/or feeling, and also the distinction between them. These will also be a matter of judgement. Accept the person's views on these as valid from their perspective. Strive to open up possible mind-sets or beliefs and ways of thinking that may lie behind the more immediate thinking of the person who is using violence in the example.

The key point from the exercise is that the violent actions which the person has used can only really be fully understood along with the thoughts and feelings that accompanied them – a triangle of behaviour. Actions are obviously the most visible part of behaviour but they are not the full part. If the person accepts this concept, then they may also begin to see that a real change in behaviour can only really occur when there have been significant changes not only in relation to actions, but also with regard to ways of thinking and dealing with emotions.

(NB: The 'thinking' and 'feelings' that have been identified in the example of violence that has been analysed may be recorded for use in future Conversations 6 and 7. This may be done in PNV Resource 7.)

The conversation may move on when the person has been able to identify and see possible relationships and connections between a person's thinking and emotions and the use of acts of violence.

Element 5 Linking my violent acts to my thinking and feelings

Ask the person to now take a few moments to bring to mind one example of their own violence that they are prepared to share and reflect on. It may already be an adjudicated matter, or an incident that is known about. If not, there is no need to share significant detail in terms of dates and location, etc. It is better if it is an occasion that the person has a good memory of, rather than one which occurred while they were heavily intoxicated or under the influence of drugs. These may be used if no other examples are available. PNV Resource 8 may be used to relate the person's own 'violence' example to the triangle of behaviour. Focus on helping the person bring out as much detail as possible in relation to their thinking and feelings before they used the violent actions. Probe and push the person to explore any ideas around entitlement or expectations about another person's behaviour that may have been somewhere in their minds. Try also to open up the range and degree of the emotions that were being felt.

It may also be helpful to the person to reflect on what was gained from their use of violence on the occasion in mind. While there may well be regret and shame, and the violence may have had negative consequences over the longer term, the gains that were present in the moment (for example, helping the person get what was wanted, reducing bodily tensions and anxiety, putting an end to an uncomfortable situation or getting someone to do or stop doing something) may also help give some hints to their thinking preceding the violence.

Point out that it is this triangle of behaviour that the person will be travelling round in several of the future conversations in trying to bring down the wall. The key message is that he or she will continue to revisit these three areas, the three points of the triangle, regularly, vigorously and powerfully. This is essential, because ultimately unless they can fundamentally change the way they think and how they are handling difficult emotional issues it is unlikely that their actions will significantly change and become safer.

(NB: The 'thinking' and 'feelings' that have been identified in the person's own example need to be recorded for use in future Conversations 6 and 7. This may be done on PNV Resource 8.)

Before concluding this element, check whether it is possible for the person to identify, even at this early stage, one different way of thinking or handling their emotions that may have prevented them from using violent actions in the example being considered.

Finally, can the person identify any possible early warning signs that may also assist in their efforts to monitor themselves in trying to stay safe in the future?

The conversation may move on when the person has been able to connect some thinking and emotional issues to an act of violence. If possible, at least one early warning sign should be identified.

Element 6 Bringing down the wall: outcomes, check-out and closure

The guidance for this element is provided on p. 59.

Reference

World Health Organisation (2004) *Preventing Violence: A Guide to Implementing the Recommendations of the World Report on Violence and Health.* Geneva: WHO.

Chapter 8

Conversation 3
My story and violence

The immediacy of the Northern Ireland conflict meant that a large proportion of its population of 1.5 million people were impacted in some ways. Many people's life stories have been bound up in what happened to them during the Troubles. This impact was differentiated in that the more socially deprived areas suffered the most, and research has identified continued trauma-related problems (Ulster University 2015).[1] In response to this reality, the Victims Commissioner has advocated for strategic efforts to ensure that the delivery of social care and criminal justice services continue to be mindful of and sensitive to the impact of the violence inflicted across society.[2]

Many men perpetrated and were at the receiving end of the violence. For some, there appeared to be a sense that this gave a certain legitimacy to the notion of violence as a way to 'solve' situations of personal or social conflict. One pioneering analysis of domestic violence in the region, tellingly called 'Hidden Violence' (Evason 1982), referred to Northern Ireland as a situation of 'armed patriarchy'. Monica McWilliams (McWilliams and McKiernan 1993), who was to become a key contributor to the Peace Process, was also involved in critical research that brought out into the open the extent of intimate partner violence that was occurring in Northern Ireland.

Conversation 3 explores with the person what has happened to them in terms of the traumas experienced in their own lives – either troubles related or arising from other significant adversities. This conversation seeks to be 'trauma aware' and sensitive to how these manifestations of abuse and violence may have played out in the person's life story and the relationship between this and moving to non-violence. Furthermore, the issues of gender and power will also be considered in terms of their relationship, if any, with the use of violence in the person's life and how they may be part of the wall blocking the path to non-violence.

Part II Promoting non-violence

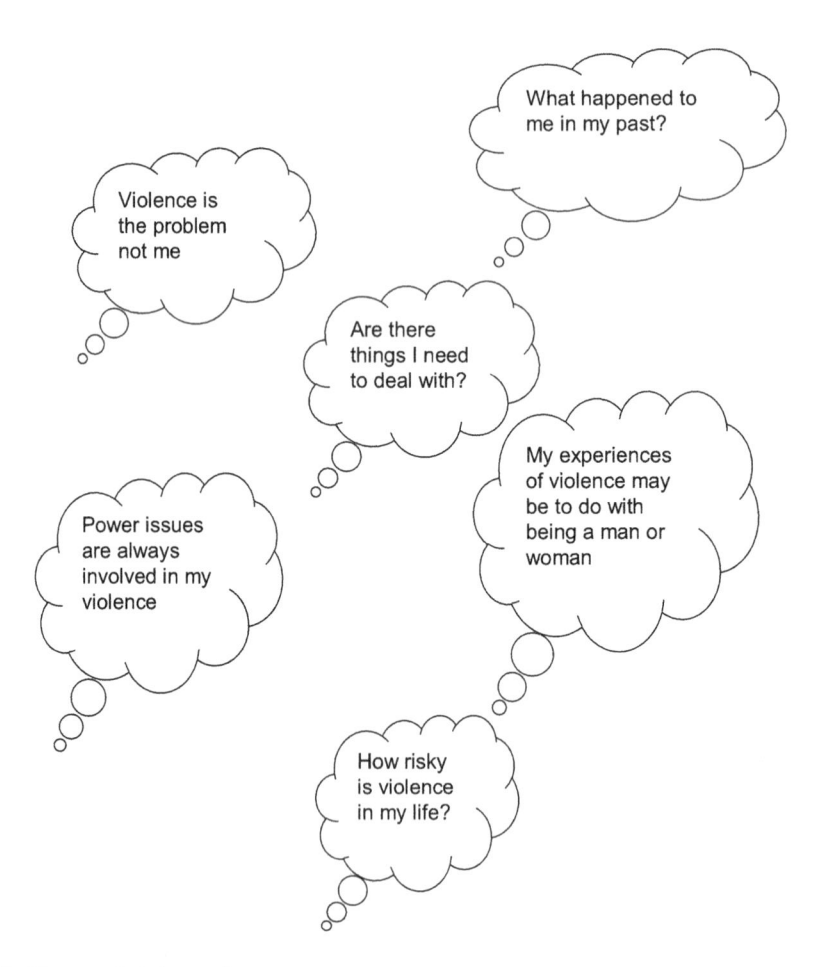

- Violence is the problem not me
- What happened to me in my past?
- Are there things I need to deal with?
- Power issues are always involved in my violence
- My experiences of violence may be to do with being a man or woman
- How risky is violence in my life?

My Story and violence: key messages

Sorting out the story of violence in my life will help me bring down the wall.

CONTENT/OBJECTIVES

1. Welcome and check-in
2. Telling the story of violence in my life
3. My use of violence and being a man or a woman
4. Power and powerlessness in my use of violence
5. Dealing with the risk of experiencing and using violence
6. Bringing down the wall: outcomes, check-out and closure

NB: Before commencing this conversation see p. 86.

Element 1 Welcome and check-in

Give a warm welcome to the person, and if following a more structured approach, begin with a reminder/summary of the person's agreed conclusions and learning outcomes from the previous meeting or full conversation.

Explain that this conversation is about the person's life story. The person will decide just how little or how much they want to disclose about past personal experiences. Specifically, the discussion will focus on the emergence and presence of violence in the person's life. It will also consider its relationship, if any, to their sex, and to issues of power and powerlessness. The conversation will conclude with where the person's story has so far left them in terms of the place of violence in their life and their view of how risky their life is currently.

The key messages may be referred to before sharing the content above so that the person knows what is going to be discussed.

Referring to guidance (see pp. 58–59) allow the person to check in.

Element 2 Telling the story of violence in my life

Ask the person to imagine a line going diagonally across the room from one corner to the other as representing their life from birth up until this point. Open up sensitively with the person when he or she first became aware of the presence of violence in life. What happened to the person in terms of becoming aware of violence, not as something the person was using but as something outside of themselves?

Alternatively, the time line may be drawn on a flip chart page, or PNV Resource 9 may be used.

Refer to the violence in the third person as a phenomenon in itself which may or may not have been present in the person's life at various points. Encourage the person to step out of the story and disassociate from what is being described, and to look in from the outside to try to pick up on the meanings that may have emerged for them in relation to encounters with violence. Respond sensitively to disclosures of violence and abuse.

Emphasise that the intention is not to pick over old wounds or hurts to deliberately disturb or distress the person. The harm caused by violence will be explored in greater depth in the next conversation. The focus for now is on reflecting on the messages and meanings that the violence may have left. In human development there is always a need to deal with past difficult events as they may continue to impact upon what will happen in the future (Leach 2014).

Ultimately, how does the person now view these experiences of violence?

Are they something that have left deep wounds and may still have some control or effect, or has the person found ways to heal the wounds.

What messages can be taken from them that may contribute to the person's efforts towards non-violence?

The conversation may move on when the person has reviewed and reflected on various aspects of the phenomenon of violence during their life.

Element 3 My use of violence and being a man or a woman

Begin this element on a light note by asking the person to list up to ten words that, in their mind, are most associated with their biological sex. Discuss the list, and pose the question that, if a person of a different sex made a list, how much similarity or difference might there be?

Point out that the discussion is right on the edge of the major and continuing controversy around the similarities and differences between men and women, and the nature of sexual identity. Agree that the conversation will only go as far as the person wishes it to go. Try to keep the focus on the person's view of the linkage, if any, between their own biological sex, their life experiences as a man or woman and their use of violence. Emphasise that there are different views on this; nothing will be imposed.

Be curious to find out about the person's perspective on this rather than to impose your own. Some ideas will be presented, but ultimately the person needs to come to their own conclusions.

Ask the person to think about a 'typical' little boy or girl aged 7 and to come up with a short list of words they would use to describe a child at this age. Encourage the person to come up with their own list but, if prompts are needed, these could include the following:

> *small – emotional – irresponsible – innocent – vulnerable – inexperienced – dependent – can cry – full of life – playful – innocent – mischievous, etc.*

Agree with the person a list that applies to them at that age. Return to their time line (PNV Resource 9), but this time focus on their own experience in growing up as a girl or a boy through the teenage years. Using some of the questions below, gently explore the process of growing into adulthood with the person.

If working with a younger person, the focus is on where he or she is on the journey to adulthood.

If Element 2 has revealed serious abuse as a young child, the above exercise will need to continue taking this into account.

Working with a man

What did this experience feel like, particularly when moving into and through his teenage years and on into his early twenties?

What sorts of expectations did he feel were placed upon him as he was growing up?

How were women referred to and talked about?

What were his experiences of put-downs and 'banter' with friends?

(If relevant, what have been his experiences of social media?)

What was his sense of having to come across as competitive, hard, tough, in control, able to take care of things, not showings feelings, not allowing himself to be vulnerable, having to hide his hurts almost like wearing a mask?

How difficult was this pressure in trying to live up to some of the above unobtainable expectations of being in control and on top of things, perhaps within the reality of few opportunities and poverty?

How did some of the above impact upon his emotions? Were there feelings of hurt, anger, jealousy, rage, depression, etc. that were blocked out or maybe sometimes exploded and resulted in violent outbursts?

How did all this impact upon how he moved into and what he expected from intimate relationships?

What beliefs has it left with him with in terms of family and fatherhood and his role within the community? What has it to do with some of the violence he may have used?

PNV 10 may also be used to reflect on how the person sees his masculinity playing out now and whether there is a need to move towards a more softer, or vulnerable, or less controlled place if he is to avoid future violence.

Working with a woman

Similarly, allow the woman to reflect on the issues which have been most specific to her sex, particularly the pressures she experienced in growing through childhood, her teenage years and into womanhood, and how she sees this.

What sorts of messages did she receive about her lack of worth and role?

What were her experiences of being pressurised and expected to behave in certain ways?

What were her experiences of bullying within relationships, family or community?

What have her experiences been on social media?

What were the expectations of her to take on caring roles?

What, if any, connections does the person make between her journey into womanhood and any issues to do with her use of violence?

Respecting diversity

The above approach reflects some of the literature in Chapter 2, which suggests that there are differences between men and women in relation to their pathways into the use of violence. In summary, the bulk of serious violence comes from men, and much of it may be connected with issues to do with masculinity and how they believe they should behave, while the much smaller amount of serious violence that comes from women appears to emerge from experiences of abuse and maltreatment.

This perspective should not be imposed on anyone. There may well be men who relate their use of violence to being previously abused and women whose violence may be more to do with issues of power and control. Throughout this element, care needs to be taken not to impose any dated stereotypes on the person. Allow each person to define their own issues in relation to gender. Support the person in striving for a complete and fully humane understanding of manhood and womanhood as the person sees it; one that gives meaning and social purpose to both. Stay curious and accept the person's conclusions as to its relationship with the use of violence.

The conversation may move on when the person has considered their experiences of growing up as a man or a woman, the messages they have taken from this, and their view as to the association between this and their use of violence.

Element 4 Power and powerlessness in my use of violence

If violence is the voice of the powerless, it is also very much the voice of the powerful. Power issues of one sort or another, as we saw in Chapter 2, are never far away in those situations where violence is taking place, and may well have already been raised and seen to be playing out in earlier parts of this conversation.

A safe way to open up the discussion on power is by drawing a large triangle (PNV Resource 11 may also be used). Agree with the person that the triangle represents a particular social or work grouping or organisation within society with which the person is familiar (e.g. a factory, a business, sports club, army, etc.). Place people who are part of the organisation along one of its sides, those with the least power at the bottom of the triangle and those with the most power at the top point.

Explore how power 'works' within the chosen group.

- If someone near the bottom is being treated badly by someone above them, is there anything that that person can do?
- How do those at the bottom communicate with those higher up?
- Do those at the top really have all the power?
- Is it better for the hierarchy in an organisation that those at the bottom are treated well and are happy, or does it matter?
- What does it depend on?
- Whose views and ways of thinking are important?, etc.

Try to bring out that, even where a traditional hierarchical organisation is chosen as an example where things should appear to be straightforward, power is nevertheless often a fluid and messy concept, and sometimes hard to pin down. How much more so may this be the case with how power plays out within relationships, families and communities?

After processing the example of power playing out within an organisation, explore with the person their experiences of power within their relationships, families or communities. How has this been – where has their position on the triangle been in relation to these areas?

Ask the person to then focus on the example of their violence that was reflected on in the previous conversation. What connections, if any, are there between this and the power issues shown on the triangle?

Finish this element by recognising that power is a reality in life. Of course, it can be a force that can lord over others to compel them to obey, something that can make a person buckle. When used in such a way, it is both violent in itself and may also bring about a violent reaction.

However, it does not necessarily have to be a negative or bad thing. Such an understanding of power is superficial. Real power is moral. There is power in truth, in patience and in doing the right thing at the right time for the right reason. Maybe in the role as a parent or with a friend the person can think of a situation in which they demonstrated a positive use of power that was for someone's good.

Encourage the person to continue to think about power issues in their life between sessions and confirm that the issue of power will be revisited in future conversations.

This conversation may move on when the person has considered and reflected on the degree to which issues of power may have been involved in their use of violence.

Element 5 Dealing with the risk of experiencing or using violence

It is possible that the previous elements may have been 'messier' than previous conversations given the sensitive, personal and contested nature of the topics, and particularly if issues of trauma have been raised. Acknowledge this reality and agree with the person to now move on.

Return the focus to the present moment and ask where the person's history, gender and experiences of power have left them in terms of how they currently experience and view the phenomenon of violence and risk.

Using PNV Resource 12 or the two corners of the room, present a continuum between two extreme and contrasting views of how people tend to see the issue of violence and risk within their lives – either total safety or total danger.

Ask the person to take a position on the continuum and their reasons for doing so.

If a person is close to, or at, the 'dangerous' end, the issue of trauma should be checked or revisited. There is also the possibility of no relationship to trauma at all. Many of the young men I have worked with have placed themselves towards the dangerous end of the continuum, as it represents the reality of life within their impoverished communities.

Again, it is about encouraging the person to step back and look at the violence as a problem that still wants to be part of their life. The person is not the violence; it is something outside of themselves. The issue for the person now is to decide what sort of relationship to have with it in going forward. The questions on PNV Resource 12 may be used to re-enforce this idea of violence as the problem – not the person.

They will also allow the person to reaffirm their goals and desires in taking forward their life in ways that do not have any relationship with violence – either as someone on the receiving end or someone who uses it. Encourage the person to identify some ideas that may assist in efforts to get safer. It may be possible, but not essential, to categorise these in terms of actions, and ways of thinking and handling feelings that the person may already be doing or new insights from the work just completed.

The conversation may move on when the person has reflected on their current association with violence and confirmed their readiness to continue working towards non-violence.

Element 6 Bringing down the wall: outcomes, check-out and closure

The guidance for this element is provided on p. 59.

Further guidance for workers on trauma and addressing the use of violence

Conversation 3 opens up the possibility for the person to share past significant trauma(s) and adversities from their lives. This will need to be addressed sensitively and compassionately. It is the person's choice and decision as to how much he or she wishes to disclose. It is also important that the person is clear that a therapeutic intervention cannot be offered through these conversations and the person should be assisted to access other appropriate services if this is an issue for them.

If there are concerns in this regard, and without trivialising the person's experience, a simple analogy of someone who has had a near-drowning experience may be used. I have a personal experience of being carried away by a wave as a child and can relate to this. After such an experience, a person will often find it difficult to go back into the water. He or she is likely to be left shocked and distressed at the time and with a fear of water. The person may be terrified to get into a swimming pool or, if they do, will never venture out of the shallow end, keeping hold of the side rail. It is not until the person has been helped or supported to talk about and overcome the dread of water that they may then be able to be taught the skills needed to swim.

The above or any similar example may be used to explore whether a person's past experiences of violence may be still casting a long shadow and continuing to be a trauma playing out for them that makes it very difficult at times to regulate their emotions or actions. Consequently, the person who has been traumatised by past experiences of abuse and violence may need to have this dealt with and healed. It may be premature and difficult to embark on making significant personal change without having addressed their trauma. If the person feels that past experiences continue to disturb them they should be offered the necessary support to do this.

It is important that the person confirms that they have worked through whatever the experiences of violence have been – and they may well have done this in their own way and using their own resources. However, if you have serious concerns, as part of the risk assessment, a psychological review of this issue with the person may need to be considered.

Notes

1 To mark the twentieth anniversary of the Good Friday (Belfast) Agreement, a further 2018 survey conducted by the Commission for Victims and Survivors showed that just over a quarter of the population continued to be affected by a Troubles-related incident.
2 Speech given by the Victims Commissioner Judith Thompson in 2016,

References

Evason, E. (1982) *Hidden Violence: A Study of Battered Women in Northern Ireland*. Belfast: Farset Co-operative Press.

Leach, P. (2014) *Family Breakdown: Helping Children Hang on to Both Their Parents*. Manchester: Unbound.

Mc Williams, M. and McKiernan, J. (1993) *Bringing it out into the Open: Domestic Violence in Northern Ireland*. Belfast: HMSO.

Ulster University (2015) *Towards A Better Future: The Trans-generational Impact of the Troubles on Mental Health*. Belfast: The Commission for Victims and Survivors.

Chapter 9

Conversation 4
The harm I have caused

Introduction

The human and social costs of the Northern Ireland conflict have been huge and unlikely to be ever fully appreciated. Nearly 4,000 people died, and many more thousands were physically and psychologically harmed. As indicated in Conversation 3, many continue to suffer from this violence. Violence was used by illegal paramilitary factions as well as by state forces. Efforts have been made to engage and help those harmed by the violence. Various truth-seeking forums and peace commissions have been proposed, including Historical Investigations units, an Independent Commission on Information Retrieval, an Independent Oral History Archive and an Implementation and Reconciliation Group. Unfortunately, these initiatives have stalled and become stuck due to continuing political disagreements. In particular, the limited acknowledgement by those who used such violence has already been described as a running sore through the peace process (Conversation 2). The sad, inescapable fact remains that many victims have been left to languish (and die) with no recognition, explanation or redress for the great harm caused by those who perpetrated the violence. Although it has many positives, the Peace Process has failed to truly address the generational and lasting hurt and trauma of those who suffered during the troubles, particularly in their quest for truth and justice.[1]

Similarly, with much common violence there is often little recognition of the harm that has been caused to those on the receiving end. The effects will often be long term and never fully erased. This conversation offers the person the opportunity (if they have not already done so) to at least begin to acknowledge and take responsibility for the harm caused. It is about exploring the empathy the person may have towards the victim(s) of their violent acts. Genuine empathy has the potential to begin to bring down the wall blocking the person's path towards non-violence.

Conversation 4: The harm I have caused

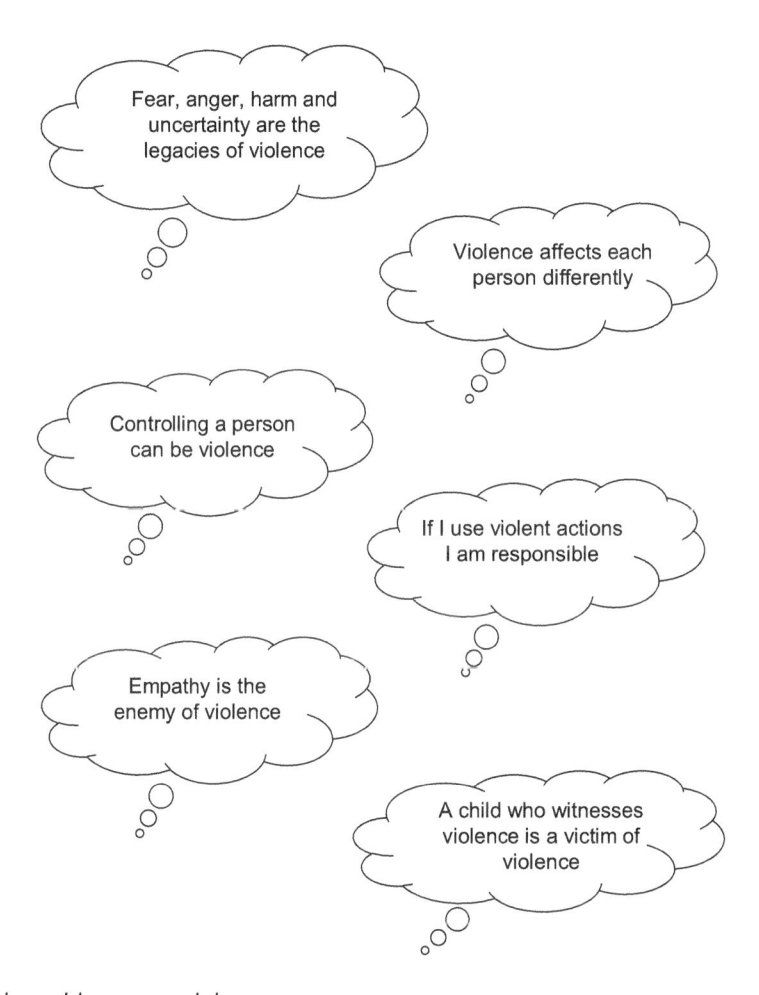

- Fear, anger, harm and uncertainty are the legacies of violence
- Violence affects each person differently
- Controlling a person can be violence
- If I use violent actions I am responsible
- Empathy is the enemy of violence
- A child who witnesses violence is a victim of violence

The harm I have caused: key messages

Taking responsibility for the harm I have caused will help me bring down the wall

CONTENT/OBJECTIVES

1. Welcome and check-in
2. Being a victim of violence
3. Harm I may have caused
4. Children and violence
5. Taking responsibility for harm caused
6. Bringing down the wall: outcomes, check-out and closure

Element 1 Welcome and check-in

Give a warm welcome to the person, and if following a more structured approach, begin with a reminder/summary of the person's agreed conclusions and learning outcomes from the previous meeting or full conversation.

Explain that this session centres on the immediate and long-term negative impacts that violence, whatever its manifestation, can have, in particular, the specific effects that the person's violent acts have had on others. The issue of the severity of the impact upon children who either experience or witness violence will also be addressed, regardless of the nature of the person's violence.

The key messages may be referred to before sharing the content above so that the person knows what is going to be discussed.

Referring to guidance on pp. 58–59 allow the person to check in.

Element 2 Being a victim of violence

Begin by asking the person to think back to their childhood. Can they remember some of the negative statements that were made to them by their parents, carers, teachers or others? A few of these could be noted; for example, you're lazy, you're stupid, you're an idiot, you're useless, etc. Briefly process the effects of these criticisms and put-downs. (For some, there may be deep wounds and a legacy of emotional pain which should be responded to sensitively.)

Move on and ask the person if they would be comfortable bringing to mind, but not to share, one specific past experience of being on the receiving end of violent actions.

Emphasise that the selected example should be one that the person can remember clearly, that it would not cause too much distress to talk about again, and does not involve the perpetrator being someone who has also been the victim of the person's own violence.

The person does not need to recount their experience of being a victim of violence. Rather, gently work through the following three questions:

1. What were the physical effects of the violence on you?
2. What were the psychological and emotional effects on you?
3. How did it affect your behaviour during the period after it happened?

PNV Resource 13 provides a summary of the multiple ways that a person may be impacted upon by violence. It also contains questions which may help the person further probe the experiences of being a victim of violence.

The conversation may move on when the person has been able to process their experiences as a victim of an incident of violence and demonstrate an understanding of the various ways it has affected them.

Element 3 Harm I may have caused

The focus now returns to the person's own example of the use of violence, which was presented in Conversation 2. PNV Resource 13 can be returned to and the three questions slowly worked through again, but this time in terms of beginning to identify some of the harm the person has caused to their 'victim'. A red pen could be used to circle the relevant affects.

There will be many variations in how people are affected by violence. These affects will be related to the type of violence used, physical force, threats and intimidation, sexually abusive, coercive controlling or psychologically/emotionally abusive behaviour. For example, exploring the effects of the physical violence used by a young person who is a gang member will have different emphases than similar work with someone who has been sending abusive and sexualised messages on social media to a teenage girl.

The core aim is to use one particular example of the person's own behaviour to help increase their understanding and ultimately their empathy. If the victim of the person's violence has been a child or a young person, as well as the effects that the person can identify from the list in PNV Resource 13, point out that there may also be negative developmental harm (discussed below). Similarly, if the issue of children being witness to the violence is raised, the degree to which they may have been negatively impacted will be returned to later to in the conversation.

The issue of a pattern or repetitive nature of the person's use of violence should also be opened up. The nature of the person's own example may allow this to be naturally explored – it is likely to be something they do often. Use the example in PNV Resource 14 to show that violent acts are rarely isolated, one-off events but may be part of a wider, sustained repetitive pattern.

Can the person's own example be viewed as fitting within a similar overall pattern of violent actions, even some mundane ones, but ultimately culminating in a process of the abuse of power and coercive control? This could be happening in different ways across a range of situations; for example, violence towards a partner, a child, a sibling, a frail parent, or cyber bullying on social media.

The conversation may move on when the person has identified and acknowledged some of the harm that may have been caused by their use of violence and also considered it within a pattern of abuse and control.

Element 4 Children and violence

If the person's use of violence has been directed towards, or witnessed by, a child or young person, then this element may be directly related to this reality. Even if there is no evidence of any involvement with children, the material should still be covered.

PNV Resource 15 may be used to briefly point out the different developmental stages that each child needs to work through to maturity. This happens best within a loving, safe, secure and nurturing environment with firm boundaries, where children are protected from all types of violence.

Highlight the fact that there is now overwhelming international evidence that experiencing significant physical, sexual or verbal/emotional abuse as a child, or growing up in an environment in which there is violence, can continue to harm children in various ways, leading ultimately to health-harming effects throughout the life course (this has already been referenced in Part I). Some of this may already be self-evident from the previous conversation and the person's own adverse childhood experiences.

A clear message should be given to the person that even just witnessing violence can have a devastating effect on children, whatever their age.

The conversation should move on when the person has demonstrated their understanding of the effects of violence on children, and, if appropriate, has identified these effects in relation to any child(ren) on the receiving end or caught up in their violence.

Element 5 Taking responsibility for harm caused

All violence leaves a legacy of some sort which cannot be undone. For some of those who have been on the receiving end of the person's violence, there may well be long-term effects for which there are no quick fixes. Point out to the person that whatever happens, whatever they do, it may well be reasonable for others to continue to feel fear and/or anger towards them. Furthermore, and not unreasonably, it may be hard for others to accept that the person can change. The previous work within this conversation should have given the person some insight into these points – if they haven't already accepted such realities. An openness to these views may be a sign of increasing empathy and understanding on the person's part of the harm caused.

Suggest to the person that a starting point may be to put on record their acknowledgement that they and no one else is responsible for the violence that has been used. PNV Resource 16 may be used to open up the discussion in relation to accepting responsibility and not hiding behind excuses and justifications. The exercise in which the person is asked to describe the violence used, but in the words of one of those on the receiving end, may demonstrate how much awareness and understanding the person has of the effects of their violent actions.

The final part of PNV Resource 16 may also be taken forward more experientially by using the corners of a room to represent the continuum – at one end are quick fixes and at the other are long-term solutions.

Where is the person on the line?

What has the person already done and what should be done to take more responsibility for what has happened?

Take the discussion further in recognising that while it may not be possible to undo all the damage that has been done by the violence, there may be some things that the person can do. The situation will rarely be completely hopeless and the person's continuing commitment to doing this personal work should be affirmed.

If the person brings up the issue of some sort of engagement with the victim(s), this can be recorded and returned to in the final conversation. As stated in Chapter 4, the outcomes of the eight conversations should contribute to the ongoing and dynamic assessing and managing of risk. Communication and connection between the person and those who have been on the receiving end of violence needs to be something that is agreed as part of the overall risk assessment, requiring the full and informed agreement of all relevant parties (see Appendix 2).

The conversation may move on when the person has accepted at least some responsibility for the use of violence and has also begun to identify and acknowledge the efforts being made to address some of the harm caused.

Element 6 Bringing down the wall: outcomes, check-out and closure

The guidance for this element is provided on p. 59.

Note

1 Political commentator Denis Bradley who was involved in efforts to address the needs of those who had suffered during the Troubles writing in the Belfast-based *Irish News* Newspaper on 2 February 2018.

Chapter 10

Conversation 5
Punching holes in my thinking towards non-violence

Fr Alec Reid (CSSR) was a crucial figure in the Northern Ireland Peace Process. He initiated the tentative communications with some of those involved in politically motivated violence to try to find alternatives to the use of violence. His role over the ensuing years has been recognised by all sides. Speaking at his funeral in 2012, the then President of Ireland Mary McAleece spoke eloquently of how he 'patiently but relentlessly punched holes in our thinking'.[1] Similarly, John Hume talked constantly about changing the language and ideas of those who were using violence. The journey from violence to peace could only be made by those who could challenge and overturn their thinking about its use. This is far from easy.

It was almost 40 years after 13 civilians were shot dead by the British army in Derry in January 1971 that the then British Prime Minister, in a powerful speech on 15 June 2010, spoke of the violence used by the soldiers on that occasion as being both 'unjustified and unjustifiable'. It was finally acknowledged that the use of violence on that occasion reflected distorted thinking and a sustained denial of the truth of the violence that was perpetrated.

In many ways, distorted and poor thinking, including particular mind-sets and beliefs, may also be seen as playing out within the minds of those who use common violence. One of the strongest findings from research is that people often see their violent actions as being necessary or justified (Alvarez and Bachman 2013). Certain ways of thinking, beliefs and mind-sets need to have holes punched in them if the person is going to knock down the wall and move towards positive change and non-violence.

Conversation 5: Punching holes in my thinking

> My thinking will influence my actions

> The human capacity for self-deception is enormous!

> The way I think is my map to take me through life – do I have the right map?

> Our brains are plastic and keep changing – no one is ever done as far as being a fixed or final person of him/herself!

> I need to focus on my thinking behind my violent actions

> The 'head' sometimes does dangerous and stupid things

Punching holes in my thinking: key messages

Getting my thinking right will help bring down the wall.

CONTENT/OBJECTIVES

1. Welcome and check-in
2. Thinking about my thinking
3. Negative thinking connected with acts of violence
4. Identifying negative thinking in my act(s) of violence
5. Moving towards new positive thinking helping me towards non-violence
6. Bringing down the wall: outcomes, check-out and closure

Element 1 Welcome and check-in

Give a warm welcome to the person and, if following a more structured approach, begin with a reminder/summary of the person's agreed conclusions and learning outcomes from the previous meeting or full conversation.

Begin the conversation by reminding the person of the triangle of behaviour and that the focus in this conversation will be on thinking and how critical the way we think is in terms of how we act. In particular, the conversation is about trying to identify positive thinking that will help with being non-violent. The point could also be made that everyone can do this – all of us can change; no one is ever a fixed or final person of him/herself.

The key messages may be briefly referred to before sharing the content above so that the person knows what is going to be discussed.

Referring to guidance on pp. 58–59 allow the person to check in.

Element 2 Thinking about my thinking

Use a simple example of three people all waiting for a bus to go to work. The bus drives past them.

One person reacts angrily and aggressively – shouting and yelling obscenities at the bus driver, arriving into work late and in an angry and aggressive mood, leading to a row with a manager and ending with nearly getting sacked.

The second person reacts differently. Rather than going into work, the person goes home in an anxious and worried state, phones in sick and misses a day's work and pay.

The third person deals more positively with the situation – contacting work to explain the situation, checking the time of the next bus, taking a pleasant walk round a nearby park while waiting for the next bus and having a normal day at work.

After briefly relating the above situation, the discussion should be on why each person reacted to the same situation in different ways. Accept any suggestions made by the person to explain the different reactions.

However, if the person has not already suggested it, ask that they consider each person's thinking about the situation as follows:

- *Person 1* – That so-and-so has driven past me on purpose, he's an ffing b! I always get treated badly and get disrespected, if anyone says anything to me in work I'll rip his head off, etc.
- *Person 2* – Oh God I'm in trouble again, everything happens to me, there's nothing I can do about this – I'm going to get into trouble at work – no one will believe me – I can't face this.
- *Person 3* – I will take a minute and think about this – maybe the bus driver is having a bad day – I don't know – I'm not going to let it ruin my day – I'll phone the bus company later. For now, I'll phone work and let them know what happened – I'll take a walk in the park and wait until the bus comes – this is a nuisance but it's not the end of the world.

The key message here is the importance of thinking in shaping a person's behaviour. While acknowledging that the brain remains a complex and only partially understood entity, what appears to happen is that when it receives a message – in this case the bus driving past – the left, more rational side of the brain processes and analyses the information. This analysis will then influence the emotional reactions.

The first person's analysis that the driver had driven past on purpose and 'for badness' led to emotions of anger and rage erupting. The second person who viewed it as yet another misfortune over which (s)he had no control led to feelings of anxiety and fear. The third person thought more critically about what was going on and how best to deal with the situation. There was no subsequent heating up of the emotions.

The point may be made that the relationship between thinking and feeling, between the heart and the mind, is even more complex, and will be returned to in Conversation 6. For now, the focus will stay with thinking.

In this regard, the bus stop example may be further explored to identify the flaws in the way in which the first two people thought at the bus stop. Some 'common' examples of bad or 'stinking' thinking may be identified below (examples of bad thinking are in italics).

Very quick and impulsive	Not taking time to consider and weigh things up
Jumping to conclusions	*'Bus driver drove past on purpose'* or *'I'm going to be in trouble in work'*
Binary (either/or)	Not open to other possibilities – for example, in limiting thinking to either the bus driver must have driven past on purpose or he didn't
Over-generalizing	*'I'm always getting treated badly'*
Expecting the worst	*'I'm going to be in trouble at work for being late'*
Not thinking of the consequences	Not considering possible outcomes from being aggressive to a manager or to taking a day off work
Blaming others	*'It's the bus driver's fault'*
Prejudiced	*'That bus driver isn't even from this country – he's useless'*

It is important to stress that everyone from time to time can fall into some of these ways of thinking – we all need to look at how we think.

To finish, can the person, and the worker, each give one example of their own bad thinking?

The conversation may move on when the person acknowledges that any of us can be limited in our thinking and that each of us needs to keep thinking critically about issues in life and to be careful of unhelpful thinking.

Element 3 Negative thinking connected with acts of violence

Agree with the person to go further to see whether it is possible to identify specific types of thinking that may be more likely to be linked with acts of violence. The impulsive, quick and no consideration for consequences-type thinking of the first passenger is an obvious example of how bad thinking could set someone on the pathway to aggression and violence.

In addition, the violence-related thinking identified in Conversation 2 and recorded on the triangles (PNV Resources 7 and 8) could be revisited. This could be recorded again on PNV Resource 17.

Similarities and differences may then be explored in relation to the list of violence-related thinking which is also outlined in PNV Resource 17. This list reflects some of the research discussed in Chapter 2.

The general point can be made that there does appear to be viewpoints, mind-sets or beliefs around entitlement, expectation and needing to have some sort of control or power that are associated with and go across the spectrum of common violence.

The metaphor of a map may be introduced. Use the example of someone being asked to find a street in Belfast but they have been given a map of Dublin to do so. How helpful is this in finding their destination? Some of the ways of thinking listed in PNV Resource 17 is the 'map' of the type of thinking that is more likely to take a person to violence.

The conversation may move on when the person has identified and can see connections between certain ways of thinking and how these may contribute in some way to acts of violence.

Element 4 Identifying negative thinking in my act(s) of violence

The point can be made that the degree of bad thinking will vary greatly among those who have used violence, and most people will not identify with every negative way of thinking now listed in PNV Resource 17. In addition, there may be more specific ways of thinking associated with the particular area of common violence that is most relevant to the person. The thinking of a young person bullying another in school will not be the same as an older man who has been controlling and abusive within relationships for many years.

Each person will have their own individual map which will have got them into varying degrees of trouble. The person now needs to go further in checking out their map. This will involve reiterating again the relevant thinking already identified from Conversation 2 as well as considering the other thinking listed in PNV Resource 17. The person should put a circle around any of the ways of thinking that apply to him or her.

This process may encourage the person to reconsider their actions described in Conversation 2 from a different perspective. Taking this further, the first four questions in Part I of PNV Resource 18 provide a different prism through which the person may also be encouraged to reconsider their original example of the use of violence. If the person is able to pull out some further examples of their bad thinking from this exercise, these should be recorded.

The conversation may move on when the person has identified and acknowledged examples of negative thinking that can be associated with their use of violence.

Element 5 Moving towards new positive thinking helping me towards non-violence

Begin this element with an assertion that despite the negative ways of thinking that have been considered, there is also a positive side to the story about thinking. Each of us has a mysterious complexity and inherent dignity (Brooks 2015, p. 224) – and the gift of human awareness. This can be presented to the person in two ways:

- The person could be asked to close their eyes for a moment or two. Imagine they are up in the corner of the room looking into their own mind to identify the thoughts they are currently having. Each person's thoughts will only be known to that person (e.g. this is the daftest thing I've ever been asked to do, or I can't wait to get home tonight, or I wonder what won the 3 o'clock at Cheltenham, or this is interesting, I am learning something here). The critical point is that not only is it just the person who knows what they are thinking, it is only him or her who can decide to do something about these thoughts as they are having them. In other words, **the gift of awareness**.
- The well-known nine-dots puzzle described on p. 101 may be used in a fun way to make a similar point. If you use the exercise and it works, you can then work with the analogy of the box representing the person's thinking up until this point and which contains the ideas that may have been linked with acts of violence. Some of these ideas may need to be cleared out of the box. However, the bigger point is that, as with the puzzle, the solution to their violence may ultimately need a completely new way of thinking outside the thinking box they have been in up until this time. If you keep thinking how you've always thought, you'll keep getting what you've always got! To do this needs **the gift of awareness**.

In moving towards the end of the conversation, the challenge for the person is to use the gift of self-awareness to really 'punch holes' in the bad thinking that has been identified, and now to be able to develop more positive thinking that may help in going towards a more positive, non-violent future.

You can now return to Part II of PNV Resource 18. This will allow the person to summarise the thinking that needs to be moved away from and more importantly the resultant new, safer thinking.

Finally, use PNV Resource 19 to see whether any other positive ways of thinking are relevant to the person and whether they feel that if they brought some of these more into their consciousness it would also help in becoming safer. Suggest that they identify a further three important ways of thinking from the list that may be relevant to them. It may be that the person's thinking already reflects one or more of the statements from the list, and this can be affirmed and reinforced.

The conversation may move on when the person has identified positive and critical thinking that he or she believes may help in their effort to be non-violent.

Element 6 Bringing down the wall: outcomes, check-out and closure

The guidance for this element is provided on p. 59.

Further general guidance for workers

From the interaction between personality and social environment, any individual may develop a cluster of unhelpful concepts and beliefs that may be associated with violent acts (Beck 1999). Particularly if the violent, controlling actions have got the person what they wanted, it is often easier to change and align the thinking with the behaviour itself. A series of justifications and rationalisations allow a person to maintain a sort of cognitive consistency between their thinking and actions. These may include blaming others, displacing responsibility, moral justifications or minimising the consequences. These are designed to convince the person that there is nothing wrong with what they have done. 'The powers of self-deception are so profound you are rarely fully honest with yourself' (Brooks 2015, p. 199).

In other words, there is no quick or easy way into another person's internal world to get them to 'fix themselves'. The process cannot be forced. Use relationship building and questioning skills to keep looking for specific and detailed information (Turnell and Edwards 1999). In line with change and motivational theory accept ambivalence, continuously reflect back and search for inconsistency between the person's explanations of their violence and its reality and how this relates to their future goals (Millner and Rollnick 2002).

Each person will have their own map that will have to be teased out. Ultimately there needs to be a shift in thinking if behavior is going to change. There is no guarantee that this will happen. All you can do is provide the opportunity for the person to consider new ways to look at the situation. There will be those who have a map that will be very difficult to modify. For example, one piece of research identified ten potential implicit ways of thinking or 'theories' held by some men who had been violent in their relationships and/or families (Gilchrist and Weldon 2012). This included thinking around the need for control, being a real man, entitlement/respect, sex drives are uncontrollable, women are objects, women are dangerous, etc. Similarly, a person who has committed a hate offence may have strong beliefs in relation to a particular group of people. Some young people who have been involved in community violence have displayed thinking that takes a hostile view of people and relationships, that you should have everything right away and that people can't be trusted, etc.

Returning to the risk issue in Chapter 4, there will be those who have a map for life that is so entrenched in dangerous thinking that substantial interventions will be required in their lives which may include more intense, focused and lengthy 'educational' programmes in addition to other criminal justice sanctions.

'Thinking outside the box' exercise

If the person is not already familiar with it, the well-known nine-dots exercise may be used in Element 5. This can be a 'fun' way to make the important point about changing our thinking to help us succeed in different areas of life.

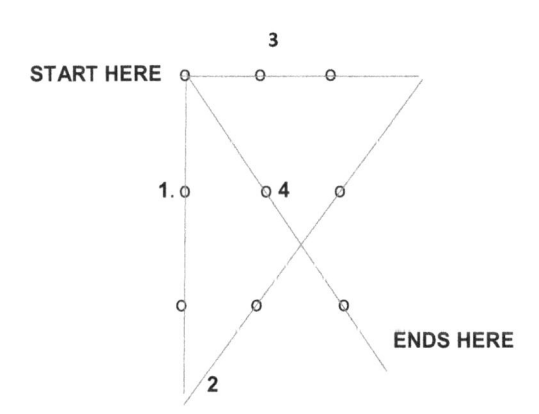

Show the person nine dots in three rows of three like in the box above (without the lines). The task is to join up all the dots but only four straight lines are allowed. Each line must join onto the next line. A new line is denoted by a change in direction. Once the first line has been started the pen can neither be lifted nor retrace itself but must keep going and go through all the dots (The solution is shown above.)

Keep it light and non-threatening: I usually point out that I couldn't do this when first shown. Like me, most people tend to think of the nine dots as a box and try to do the puzzle within the outline of the box shape. The breakthrough in thinking that is required for the task is to not feel restrained to keep the lines all in the box – thinking outside the box!

Note

1 Fr Alex Reid made an extraordinary contribution to the Northern Ireland Peace Process. From the religious community deeply rooted in the area of Belfast in which I worked as a Probation Officer he reached out to those using violence and worked incessantly for peace. He is the priest in the iconic and terrible photograph, praying over the body of one of the two British soldiers who had just been murdered after driving into a paramilitary funeral.

References

Alvarez, A. and Bachman, R. (2013) *Violence The Enduring Problem* (2nd edn). London: Sage.

Beck, A. (1999) *Prisoners of Hate: The Cognitive Basis of Anger, Hostility and Violence.* New York: Harper Collins.

Brooks, D. (2015) *The Road to Character.* London: Allen Lane.

Gilchrist, E. and Weldon, S. (2012) Implicit Theories in Intimate Partner Violence Offenders. *Journal of Family Violence*, 27(8).

Millner, W.R. and Rollnick, S. (2002) *Motivational Interviewing: Preparing People for Change.* London: The Guilford Press.

Turnell, A. and Edwards, S. (1999) *Signs of Safety: A Solution and Safety Oriented Approach to Child Protection Casework.* New York: W.W. Norton & Company.

Chapter 11

Conversation 6
Dealing with feeling and non-violence

In Chapter 1 I remembered a colleague describing those who justified the use of violence as 'smiling assassins' (p. 15). The implication was of cold, calculating, emotionless people who could calmly carry out the worst atrocities. There may have been some people like that, but many outbursts of violence throughout the Troubles were fuelled by emotionally charged reactions to events – erupting out of anger, outrage, fury, hate, despair or whatever.

John Rusesabagina (2000) lived through the horrific genocide and violence that occurred in Rwanda in the 1990s. He has also asserted that many violent acts were based on emotion. As he put it, perpetrators of the most terrible violent acts would justify them later with whatever facts they could 'scrounge up'. John Hume, as well as constantly challenging people's thinking, also recognised that there was a messy mix of 'hearts and minds', both of which needed to be addressed in the journey to peace and non-violence.

Emotion plays its part within many acts of common violence – anger, shame, humiliation, frustration and others are often associated with acts of aggression. This conversation allows the person to explore the place of emotion within their own situation. It reflects the wisdom of the ages, affirmed by modern psychology that emotional regulation and intelligence will be critical in contributing to more balanced and safer lives for us all (Goleman 2004). In other words, the wall will only start to come down when both the heart and the mind are working together in journeying towards non-violence.

- My heart can be a riotous mix of feelings and emotions
- I need to deal with how I feel
- If I bury my feelings I bury them alive
- My feeling are my own and unique to me
- Too much or too little emotion may affect my thinking
- Can I separate immediate action from emotion?
- I need to bring my thoughts and feelings together to have better balance in my life

Dealing with feeling and non-violence: key messages

Dealing better with my emotions will help me bring down the wall.

CONTENT/OBJECTIVES

1. Welcome and check-in
2. Owning my feelings
3. Anger and my use of violence
4. Emotions and my use of violence
5. Managing my emotions in getting safer
6. Bringing down the wall: conclusions, check-out and closure

Element 1 Welcome and check-in

Give a warm welcome to the person, and if following a more structured approach, begin with a reminder/summary of the person's agreed conclusions and learning outcomes from the previous meeting or full conversation.

In introducing the conversation, point out that emotions or feelings can play a significant part in any area of behaviour and this is no different with violence. The conversation will explore how important it is for each of us to be open and to talk about our emotional life and particularly those emotions which we find difficult and may have some association with the use of violence. Agree that to keep things straightforward the words *feeling* and *emotion* will be treated as the same.

The key messages can be briefly referred to before sharing the content above so that the person knows what is going to be discussed.

Referring to guidance on pp. 58–59 allow the person to check in.

Element 2 Owning my feelings

Point out that there is no universal agreement on the precise nature of our emotional life. For example, there is as yet no single agreed comprehensive list of exactly what makes up the emotions (Ekman 1999). Allowing for this reality, ask the person to take a few minutes to make a list of as many feelings or emotions that they know the words for. If the person is struggling, reference can be made back to the various feelings and emotions that have been mentioned in some of the elements within earlier conversations, particularly Conversation 2.

PNV Resource 20 may then be shared. Acknowledge every emotion that the person has identified as well as those in the Resource sheet. Make the general point that you yourself, as well as every other human being on the planet, has felt every feeling on the lists at some point in their lives. However, each human being experiences emotion in a unique way; each person has their own emotional fingerprint like no other person.

The seven statements in the same Resource can then be slowly worked through as a summary of current ideas about the emotions and also how best to deal with our emotional lives. The person does not have to accept all the points but should reflect on their view of each of them.

Move the discussion on to the two questions in PNV Resource 20, exploring the difficult issues of the person blocking or repressing any emotions and also those that the person most associates with their use of violence.

The conversation may move on when the person has identified and reflected on the emotions and has identified some that they find difficult and some which may be related in some way to their use of violence

Element 3 Anger and my use of violence?

Agree with the person to focus on anger to begin with. The other emotions that the person has associated with their use of violence can be returned to shortly. Even if anger has not been on the person's list, which is highly unlikely, time should be taken with the person to explore it.

As with the emotions in general, there are differing views about anger. The approach taken is that anger is a natural, normal emotion that we all experience. Moreover, it can be 'an essential part of who we are, vital to our survival in that we need anger to define boundaries' (Pert 1997, p. 285).

Anger is also an emotion that all of us need to learn to deal with both in terms of the amount of anger we may experience and also how we may then express it. 'To learn to handle our anger is a complex task which usually cannot be completed before adulthood, or even mid-life, and which is often never completed' (Peck 1980, p. 67).

Take the person through the six-stage model outlined in PNV Resource 21 (Novaco 1976). While doing this, ask the person to revisit, in their own mind, the example of violence shared in Conversation 2 (PNV Resource 8).

(If the person does not feel anger was present in this example, ask them to think about another situation where anger got the better of them, and led to some sort of outburst. The person does not have to share this example; they can work with it in their own head).

Once the person is clear about the example of behaviour they will refer to, begin at the first stage of the model in PNV Resource 21. Work slowly through the stages, allowing the person to see whether there were any connections between their own experience and the model as it is outlined. In particular, how did their thinking and mind-sets relate to the triggering and building up of their anger? Can the person get a sense of what was fuelling the anger, and how it moved, slowly or quickly, towards the outburst? These points may be recorded for later in the conversation.

The following questions may also be used to further probe into the anger outburst considered in Resource 21.

- How frequently are such outbursts occurring?
- How quickly does the person move up towards the outburst?
- How serious or dangerous are the violent outbursts that occur at 'crisis point'?
- In what areas of their life is it causing problems – is it only happening within certain situations or relationships? If so, what may be the deeper roots to the violence other than mismanaged anger?
- How bad are the 'dips'?

If anger and rage issues do appear to be a major feature of the person's life, then, if not already done so in Conversation 3, a possible association with past traumas should be gently explored. 'Anger and trauma have an intriguing relationship' (Novaco and Chemtob 1998, p. 167). There may also be a need for a more focused therapeutic anger management programme which may be returned to in deciding how to go forward after the final conversation.

The conversation may move on when the person has considered the role of anger within their use of violence.

Element 4 Emotions and my use of violence

Ask the person to go a little further into other emotions associated with their example of the use of violence and which may have been behind or been less obvious than the anger.

One way into this if working with a man is to share the findings from a piece of research carried out into the relationship between emotional issues and violence (Umberson et al. 2003). It involved two groups of men. One of the groups was made up of men who were known to use violence in their relationships. The other group contained men who were known not to be violent. Both groups were asked to keep a structured diary over a two-week period mainly about the state of their emotions. Interestingly, most of the men who did not use violence reported difficulties and deterioration in their own emotional state when they experienced some stress in their relationships, particularly if they felt that their personal control was being challenged or reduced. On the other hand, the men who used violence were more likely to report no significant emotional changes, turmoil or disturbance in their own feelings of control in response to stress or conflict within their relationships.

Reflect with the person why this may be before sharing the conclusion from the researchers.

The suggestion from the study was that it was not the difficult emotions by themselves that were related to the violence; rather the repression or denial of such emotions increased the likelihood of them being acted out in aggressive outbursts. One man in the study described how he responded when his partner demanded to know how he felt: 'I kicked her off the couch and shouted "this is how I feel".' The non-violent men, although appearing to be struggling with their emotions, were at least able to have more awareness of them and were better at regulating their actions. Someone who is more aware of their feelings may be able to reflect on and think about them, and possibly talk about them in some way rather than just acting them out.

Take the person through questions 1 and 2 (in the boxes) in PNV Resource 22 and process this further.

Whether the above study is used within the conversation or not, push the person to try to identify the emotions that may have been playing out. As well as anger, were there other feelings to do with shame or humiliation coming from a perceived loss of control or loss of face? Were these possibly the driving force for the anger and aggression?

If anger did not appear to be associated with the person's use of violence, what was going on emotionally – excitement, arousal, feelings of having power?

In whatever way the emotions may have been playing out destructively in the situation, how would the person answer Question 2 in trying to identify ways in which these could have been dealt with better?

NB: Do not address Question 3 on the Resource Sheet yet.

The conversation may move on when the person has explored and made some connection between their emotions and their example of violence.

Element 5 Managing my emotions and getting safer

Point out that there remain differing views on the primacy of emotional or rational reactions in how human beings respond to the situations that they encounter. To further illustrate this phenomenon, ask the person to close their eyes for a few moments and imagine they are in the following situation:

> *You are walking up a dark alley which is poorly lit. You suddenly hear a loud noise. You instantly freeze, your heart starts to race, you feel goose pimples all over, your mouth goes dry, your stomach churns, and you rapidly turn to face the source of the noise. You will not be thinking with the left side of your brain – it will have been overruled by the emotional right brain! This is an emotional hijack. The brain has sensed danger and has alerted the emotional side first. Even as you continue to walk up the alley you will find it hard to shake off the sense of unease and danger. Even though you see a cat coming out of the darkness where the noise came from and you know there is no danger, you still find it difficult to stop your emotions taking over.*

This is a simple example of where, in responding to external stimuli, emotions may come before intellectual awareness. Certainly, within anxiety-provoking or other high-stress situations as in the dark alley, it is unlikely that most people will be able to avoid emotions coming to the fore and taking over.

The relationship between thinking and feeling is complex and will vary from person to person, and it is not all to do with the context. Emotions may well come from a person's intellectual awareness and thinking but sometimes they may come before it. Without getting too bogged down in the science, it can be pointed out that there continues to be much uncertainty as to the precise relationship between thoughts and feelings, between the mind and the heart. They are complex and not yet fully understood. Arguments still go on as to the precise degree to which we decide everything using our rational brain or our feelings and emotions. The key point is that there appears to be some sort of two-way cross-talk and feedback between the two respective areas of the brain. 'Feelings and thoughts are as inseparable as two sides of the same coin' (Meehan 2000, p. 9).

A simple metaphor can help bring the concept to life. A bird needs two wings to fly and both wings need to work in relationship to each other.

Similarly, to stay safe we need to have our thinking and our feeling both working well and both in relationship to each other. We need to combine them both. – to bring thinking and feeling together to have better balance, judgement and wisdom (Covey 2004).

This is not straightforward, nor does it happen immediately. It takes us to be well into our twenties to allow our rational and emotional brains to be both fully mature and to be able to work well together; in other words, the gift of awareness referred to in the previous conversation.

The developmental reality that the human brain is not fully formed until one's mid- twenties should be addressed sensitively with younger people. Their emotions are likely to be well developed from an early age and they can be helped to talk about and become more aware of these emotions. This may be helpful for feelings like anger, fear or sadness. The reality that these may feel overwhelming at times can be explored and accepted. The fact that the rational side of the brain will not develops fully until their mid-twenties and will be much quieter can be acknowledged. The young person can still be encouraged to focus on the particular types of violent actions that need to be moved away from and supported in their efforts towards change.

Revisit PNV Resource 22 and spend time on the critical issue raised in Point 3. In reflecting further on their use of violent actions, to what degree can the person see that, at its core, there was some sort of desire for entitlement and power?

Furthermore, this desire, need or inclination was present in both their thinking and their feelings. Can the person recognise this and begin to identify ways to move away from it towards non-violence?

PNV Resources 23(i) and 23(ii) contain some further ideas on 'emotional intelligence', including an 'emergency relaxation' tool which may be referred to and used if appropriate.

The conversation may move on when the person feels they have identified some ideas in better managing the emotional content of their violent acts.

Element 6 Bringing down the wall: outcomes, check-out and closure

The guidance for this element is provided on p. 59.

References

Covey, S. (2004) *The 8th Habit: From Effectiveness to Greatness*. London: Simon & Schuster.

Ekman, P. (1999) Basic Emotions. In Dagleish, T. and Power, T. (eds), *The Handbook of Cognition and Emotion*. Chichester, Sussex: John Wiley & Sons.

Goleman, D. (2004) *Destructive Emotions and How We Can Overcome Them*. London: Bloomsbury.

Meehan, J. (2000) *Reasons have Hearts Too*. Texas: Thomas More Publishing.
Novaco, R.W. (1976) The Functions and Regulation of the Arousal of Anger. *American Journal of Psychiatry*, 133: 10.
Novaco, R.W. and Chemtob, C.M. (1998) Anger and Trauma: Conceptualisation, Assessment and Treatment. In Follette, V.M., Ruzek, J.I. and Abueg, F.R., *Cognitive Behavioural Therapies for Trauma*. London: The Guilford Press.
Peck, M.S. (1980) *The Road Less Travelled*. London: Arrow.
Pert, C.B. (1997) *The Molecules of Emotion: Why You Feel the Way You Feel*. London: Simon & Schuster.
Rusesabagina, P. (2000) *An Ordinary Man: The True Story Behind Hotel Rwanda*. London: Bloomsbury.
Umberson, D., Anderson, K.L., Williams, K. and Chen, M.D. (2003) Relationship Dynamics, Emotion State and Domestic Violence: A Stress and Masculinities Perspective. *Journal of Marriage and Family*, 65(1): 233–247.

Chapter 12

Conversation 7
Conflict, power and non-violence

The historical roots of the recent Northern Ireland Troubles and conflict can be measured in centuries. The degree to which this resulted in or came from abuses of power continues to be argued about. Nevertheless, the Good Friday (or Belfast) Agreement, an international treaty between Britain and the Republic of Ireland, provided a powerful example of conflict resolution and respect for diversity. As one commentator stated, it brought to an end the longest and most vicious internal conflict in the history of the United Kingdom.[1] Of course, conflict and disagreement remain. In the words of one Northern Ireland politician, the difference is that in the past the situation was difficult and bloody; now it is just difficult because the bloodshed has gone.[2] (The extent of the difference is illustrated by the failure to even agree on the name of the Treaty mentioned above.)

Nevertheless, those who constructed the Agreement saw at its heart the attempt to find ways to share rather than abuse power in the relationship between the two main communities in Northern Ireland. John Hume and David Trimble, as representatives of both of these communities, worked together to model this sharing of power, for which they shared the Nobel Peace Prize. They strove together for a process that eschewed ideas of engaging in violence, be it verbal, physical or of any type. These are all abuses of power and will not resolve conflict.

Similarly, conflict is an issue for individuals in their relationships, families and communities. These conflicts can often be difficult and divisive. The person needs to consider their use of violence within the context of conflict, and in particular its relationship with abusing their power. Furthermore, if the conflict is ultimately arising from the person's abuse of power, then this is the primary issue that needs to be faced. Concentrating only on the conflict that emerges from an underlying abuse of power will prove ineffective. Ultimately, until power is handled safely, the wall blocking the way to non-violence will stay up.

Part II Promoting non-violence

- Conflict is normal and persistent
- Conflict can be one of the most difficult problems in life
- Some conflicts never get sorted out
- Conflict may come from or lead to an abuse of power and violence
- Some violence may be all to do with abusing power and nothing to do with conflict
- Do I need to find safer ways to handle conflict?
- Sometimes conflicts can be necessary and healthy

Conflict, power and non-violence: key messages

Dealing better with conflict in my life will help me bring down the wall.

CONTENT/OBJECTIVES

1. Welcome and check-in
2. My responses to conflict
3. 'Character contests' and 'loss of face' in conflict
4. Ideas on dealing with conflict non-violently
5. Is my violence about power, conflict, or both?
6. Outcomes, check-out and closure

Element 1 Welcome and check-in

Give a warm welcome to the person, and if following a more structured approach, begin with a reminder/summary of the person's agreed conclusions and learning outcomes from the previous meeting or full conversation.

Point out that conflict can be built in, normal and persistent within some of our relationships with partners and ex-partners, families, work situations, as well as within communities. It can be very difficult. If the person has mentioned conflict situations within their check-ins, this should be acknowledged. This conversation will allow the person to begin to explore relevant issues for them in relation to conflict, and its association, if any, with their use of violence as well as issues of power.

The key messages may be briefly referred to before sharing the content above so that the person knows what is going to be discussed.

Referring to guidance on pp. 58–59, allow the person to check in.

Element 2: My responses to conflict

Open up the topic by asking the person to take part in a brief exercise to get them thinking about how they tend to deal with conflict in general.

Agree the ground rules – stand up, about 2 metres apart facing each other, no talking and no physical contact during the 30 seconds of the short exercise.

Ask the person to take a few seconds to imagine you as a major conflict in their life.

The conflict you represent is about to come at the person, right now, this minute!

When it does so, ask the person to show their normal 'reaction' in dealing with it, but to do this only by their body movement, posture, positioning in the room, stance, proximity to you, etc.

Then as the 'conflict', in silence, start to move slowly towards the person.

Thank the person, sit down again and then process what they did in terms of whether they moved closer or further away from the conflict or didn't move at all. How aggressive or passive was the response? How quick or slow? How much thought?

Don't overplay the exercise but point out that you have been trying to get a sense of the person's 'default' position in a conflict.

Using PNV Resource 24, point out that 'it is normal to feel conflict in our bodies' (Savage and Boyd-Macmillan 2010, p. 40). An automatic physiological reaction takes effect as referred to in the resource. The immediate urge towards freeze, flight or fight may also be viewed as a tendency towards either more aggressive or passive responses.

Once again, for a more experiential feel, the two corners of a room may be used to represent the two extreme positions.

The conversation should explore the potential long-term consequences for those who go too much towards either extreme.

Point out the dangers for the person who constantly comes at conflicts by being aggressive and making sure no one walks over them. It may appear to be positive to begin with, but what damage may it do to relationships both in the short and in the long run? Could it also get the person into trouble?

Similarly, with the person who keeps trying to avoid or withdraw from conflicts, where might this end up in terms of their relationships or when the pressure cooker finally explodes?

The person could be asked to place themselves on the continuum and whether they are happy where they are. If not, what direction do they want to move in and how far have they to go?

The issues of different responses to different conflict situations could also be explored. What does the fact that the person has the ability to make different choices say? What is influencing their choice? What does this say about the power the person may have within any situation?

The conversation may move on when the person has reflected on their conflict style and accepts the danger of an extreme position in either way and has also considered the issue of different responses.

Element 3 'Character contests' and 'loss of face' in conflict

Inform the person that many situations of conflict can arise very quickly from the most ordinary and mundane interactions.

Whether it is in a bar, on the road or in a family home, a school, a workplace or whatever, sometimes conflicts may break out, and within seconds there can be a senseless rush towards aggression and violence.

What appears to happen is that whatever may have sparked the initial conflict is soon overtaken by something else. It is a rush through the stages of a 'character contest', as shown in PNV Resource 25 (see also Chapter 3, pp. 39–40). Rather than being about the original 'incident', the issue becomes one of regulating aroused emotions, particularly in warding off feelings of shame and humiliation, and the protection of reputation around the potential perceived 'loss of face' in that moment. This can be almost irresistible, particularly for the first 90 seconds or so.

The person may also consider the 'compass of shame' on the same Resource, and again where they tend to default to in those situations and where they have felt slighted or disrespected and experienced loss of face (Nathanson 1992).

The question for the person is if they get caught up in such conflicts, are they able to bring their learning from the previous two conversations in terms of being able to step back, think and manage their emotions better and not rush towards using violence? This may be particularly difficult for a young person, given the developmental issues referred to in Conversation 6.

These types of conflicts may have already come up in the person's check-in at the beginning of previous conversations or sessions. Important messages about trying to think more positively and manage aroused emotions may have already been explored. If appropriate, return to one of the person's examples of conflict, particularly if it is ongoing and pernicious, and rehearse with the person how violence may be avoided.

The conversation may move on when the person has considered whether such quick-fire conflicts are an issue in their life. If so, can the person recognise the emotional nature of these conflicts and the need to manage them?

Element 4 Ideas on dealing with conflict non-violently

The point can be made that while there is a massive amount of literature and study into the best ways to handle conflict there are no straightforward answers. Rather than just present a list of rules or guidelines, an example of a conflict is used to bring the issue to life, and relate the guidance to.

Share the scenario between Pat and Frankie as outlined in PNV Resource 26. Allow the person a little time to reflect on their response to the conflict situation described. This may be noted down in the Resource.

The person does not have to share their 'response' immediately. Agree that, if not written down, it can be kept in the person's mind as you work through the ideas on PNV Resource 27. They are not being imposed but just put forward as ideas that have been shown to be useful in managing conflict.

While each of the five ideas can be thoroughly discussed, the importance of communication within conflict should be emphasised. Points 2 and 3 from PNV Resource 27 represent the essence of the two 'golden rules' of conflict resolution: 'seek first to understand and then be understood' (Covey 2015). They have underpinned most of the peace initiatives throughout the world, including Northern Ireland, and apply to all types of conflict.

Point 2 is about the absolutely vital role of listening within any conflict. The person may have come up with a range of useful responses to Frankie in the scenario; for example, advising, negotiating, problem-solving, criticising, etc. Acknowledge that their ideas all have their place. Ask the person to think about the extent to which their own approach involved trying to first of all listen to Frankie and to seek to understand his views and feelings. (Some possible examples of this type of more reflective listening are given on the resource sheet.)

This is the type of listening needed within conflict, particularly if the conflict is between those who are in some sort of relationship. The underlying and powerful message that such listening gives is that the other person is valued; they are important. It may be meeting one of a human being's deepest needs to be understood. If the person can do this, they will be demonstrating one of the most important skills in life (Covey 2006, p. 191). Emphasise that what is being proposed is not some sophisticated or unnatural counselling technique. In fact, it is more about having the will power and the patience to be prepared to listen. The good news is that if the person really wants to listen to another person, and even if they forget all the guidance and 'tips,' they will still be able to do it.

The other critical aspect of communication within conflict for the person to consider is the way in which we get our own side of the conflict across. Give a brief reminder of Conversation 4 when the person was asked for a list of the put-downs they may have experienced in growing up and how hurtful they were. This needs to be borne in mind in terms of trying to make our position clear in a conflict, in a way that does not attack, blame or put down the other person. Again, the resource sheet includes some examples of the sorts of 'I' statements required in getting our position across without abusing the other person.

Being able to hold our own ground, to hold onto what we believe is right, while at the same time respecting and accepting the contrasting views of another, lies at the heart of conflict resolution. However, as Point 5 makes clear, some conflicts will never be resolved and the difficult challenge is to find a way to agree to disagree.

The conversation may move on when the person has considered and understood the five key ideas in relation to conflict and related them to conflict within their own life.

Element 5 Is my violence about power, conflict, or both?

Begin this element by agreeing that Pat and Frankie were eventually able to reach some sort of agreement between each other and to resolve their conflict without violence. Pat, as parents often have to do, used power to safeguard Frankie, a young person, from harm. The conflict was necessary. Pat could not give in to Frankie. Neither did Pat want to give up on Frankie either. This was a positive example of the use of power and the resolution of a conflict.

However, point out that issues of power and conflict do not often get sorted out so well. Using PNV Resource 28 and its five circles, work through how they are often associated with violence.

1   First, it would also have been very easy for Pat to have crossed the line into being violent towards Frankie in their conflict. Share another example of John, a father who was in conflict with his daughter Jo, aged 15. He worried about her contacting strangers on the internet and was anxious to protect her. When he discovered that she met a 24-year-old

Conversation 7: Conflict, power and non-violence

man following contact on social media, John flew into a rage, smashed Jo's i-phone, struck her across the face and verbally threatened and abused her. Circle 1 in Resource 28 represents those situations when someone abuses their power and uses violence, even though that person may be trying to do the right thing.

2   Continue by suggesting that Frankie could also have become violent and refused to accept the wise parental guidance from Pat. Circle 2 in Resource 28 refers to violence by those in situations where they do not accept the legitimate rights of the other person's position and seek to use their own power to undermine this.

3   Emphasise that the abuse of power, that one is not entitled to, is in reality violence. To do this by controlling another person will also often trigger conflict. The reality that a person's coercive attitudes, expectations and actions have triggered the conflict in the first place may sometimes get lost within the ensuing turmoil. Circle 3 represents those situations in which the misuse of power also leads to conflict and more violence.

4   Of course, power may also be abused in more subtle ways without leading to conflict. Mark, aged 25, built up a relationship with a 14-year-old girl who was in care. There was no conflict in the relationship. Mark was grooming the young person because he wanted to be sexual with her. He was manipulating her and using violence towards her. Circle 4 represents such exploitative violence.

5   Make the point that thus far, the circles have all begun with the issue of power. They mostly highlight how violence has its roots in the misuse of power which then often plays out in conflict. However, there will also be those situations in which every-day, mundane life pressures and circumstances will create tension and conflict. They will not initially involve overt power dynamics playing out. They will lead to friction and turmoil. Of course, the inability to handle such conflict safely may then lead to one or other of the parties abusing power through the use of some type of violence within the conflict. This conflict-dominated violence is represented in Circle 5.

Linking the above examples with Resource 28, encourage the person to reflect on the deeper aspects of the example of their own use of violent actions. At their heart, does the person have expectations to which ultimately they are not entitled and which are designed to control? In some ways, is the person's behaviour seeking to undermine the character, the identity, the integrity and the personhood of others? It is important for the person to consider the roots to their own use of violence and try to bring out into the light the negative power dynamics, however subtle, which may be playing out and how their own violence is connected to issues of power and powerlessness.

The importance of the relationship that the person has experienced with you as the worker is relevant to this conversation. You may have some appropriate power over the person. You will have modelled the use of your power through respectful dialogue, listening and sharing ideas and perspectives, including disagreements, throughout the previous conversations.

The conversation may move on when the person has concluded the degree to which conflict and/or power issues are related to their decisions to use violence.

Element 6 Bringing down the wall: outcomes, check-out and closure

The guidance for this element is provided on p. 59.

Notes

1 Fintan O'Toole writing in the *Irish Times* (25 February 2018) preparing to mark the twentieth anniversary of the Good Friday (Belfast) Agreement in the same year.
2 In an article in the *Irish News* (a Belfast morning newspaper), Deadan De Bréadún reported the referred-to comments made by a Northern Ireland MP at a meeting in relation to ongoing talks about the stuttering Peace Process.

References

Covey, S. (2006) *The 7 Habits of Highly Effective People*. London: Simon & Schuster.
Nathanson, D.L. (1992) *Shame and Pride*. New York: Norton.
Savage, S. and Boyd-Macmillan, E. (2010) *Conflict in Relationships: At Home, At Work, In Life*. Oxford: Lion.

Chapter 13

Conversation 8
Keep on keeping on towards non-violence

The Northern Ireland Peace Process, particularly in terms of how to respectfully share power between the two communities, has been torturous and protracted and, in some ways, will never be complete. Even though paramilitary (and state) violence has greatly diminished, it has not been eliminated. For example, during the period 2007 until 2015 there were 22 murders, over 1,000 shootings and bombings, 780 punishment attacks, thousands of people in paramilitary groupings and nearly 4,000 families forced to move from their homes.[1] Even where paramilitary organisations have been officially wound down, the informal authority and abuse of power by certain key figures has, in some cases, been sustained, despite the 'official rhetoric of transition' (Bean 2007).

Since the Good Friday (Belfast) Agreement, there have been further negotiations and agreements. At the time of writing, it is the twentieth anniversary of the agreement. There is stalemate in terms of how best to share power. Fr Reid (a critical figure in initiating the process and mentioned in Conversation 3) often used the phrase 'keep on keeping on' in encouraging those to stay on the journey towards non-violence.

'Keep on keeping on' will often be what the person who is striving to move away from the use of common violence will have to do. This is what the final and continuing conversation is about. Change is always difficult. It is rarely a cut-and-dried matter. Progress can be slow and painstaking, and the pressure and opportunity to abuse power will never disappear. This conversation is about recognising this reality and affirming the commitment the person has made thus far and building on this in terms of how best to 'keep on keeping on' in finally removing the wall and moving towards non-violence and their own specific goals in life.

Part II Promoting non-violence

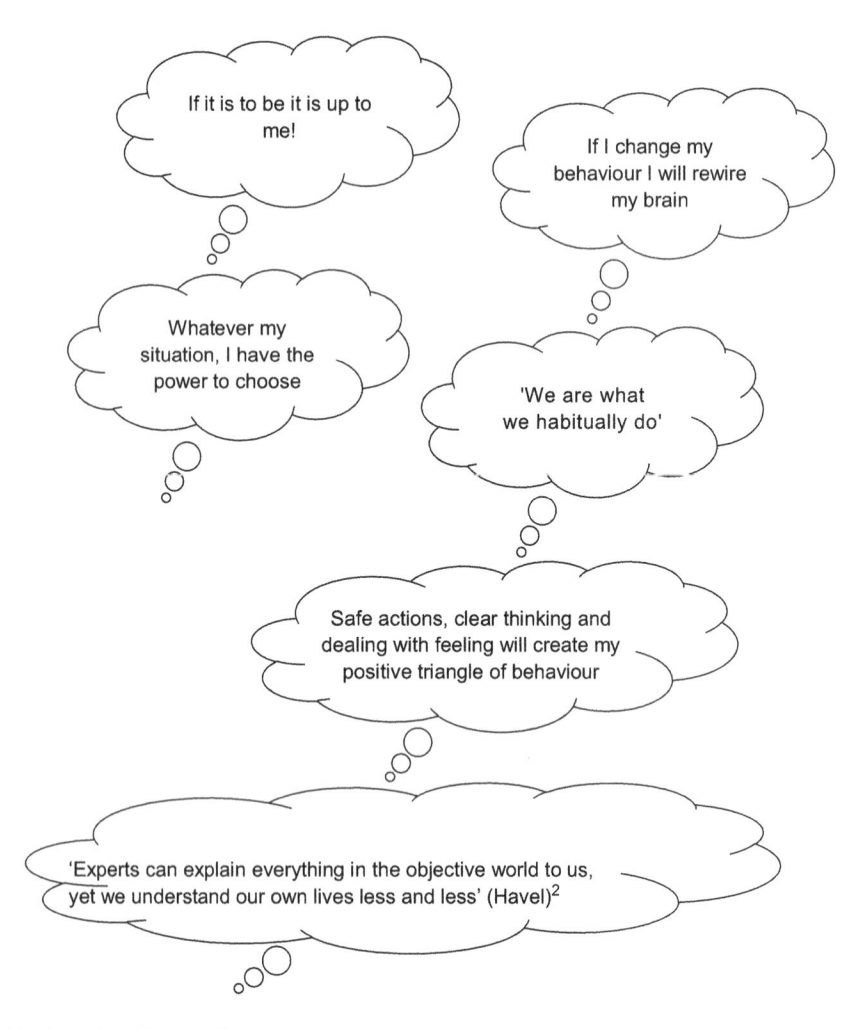

- If it is to be it is up to me!
- If I change my behaviour I will rewire my brain
- Whatever my situation, I have the power to choose
- 'We are what we habitually do'
- Safe actions, clear thinking and dealing with feeling will create my positive triangle of behaviour
- 'Experts can explain everything in the objective world to us, yet we understand our own lives less and less' (Havel)[2]

Keep on keeping on: key messages

I am determined to now go forward and bring down the wall blocking my way to non-violence.

CONTENT/OBJECTIVES

1. Welcome and check-in
2. Reviewing my learning
3. Awareness and the power to choose
4. My strengths and staying safe
5. Moving towards my positive 'triangle' of behaviour
6. Ending: is the wall down and will it stay down?

Element 1 Welcome and check-in

Give a warm welcome to the person, and if following a more structured approach, begin with a reminder/summary of the person's agreed conclusions and learning outcomes from the previous meeting or full conversation.

Given that this is the final conversation, it is a good time to step back, recognise and review the important personal work the person has done. Where has this left them in terms of their behaviour and how they want to go forward – will it be worth it and what does the person need to do to bring the wall down and 'keep on keeping on'?

The key messages may be referred to before sharing the content above so that the person knows what is going to be discussed.

Referring to guidance on pp. 58–59 allow the person to check in.

Element 2 Reviewing my learning

Using PNV Resource 29, revisit each of the previous conversations and agree once again the outcomes that the person has taken from these – these may have already been recorded when completing each of the conversations.

The conversation may move on when the person has reviewed and summarised their conclusions and learning from the work done during the previous conversations.

Element 3 Awareness and the power to choose

Emphasise that it is very easy for any of us to get drawn into our own little worlds and to have only a limited awareness of the bigger picture of our lives and our behaviour. Affirm the person for having taken this period of time over the previous weeks/months to step back and think critically about who they are, what they are and what they are doing, particularly in relation to the place of violence within their life.

The negative use of power has been a theme throughout the conversations and how it is often played out in one way or another within acts of violence. In this final conversation, the onus is on a more positive understanding of the use of power. This may be illustrated by the well known story of someone who was able to make a positive choice despite facing the most difficult circumstances.

> *Viktor Frankl was born in Vienna. In 1942, he was deported to the concentration camp in Theresiendstradt and spent the next three years in extermination camps, among them Auschwitz and Dachau. His parents, his fiancée and other close relatives all perished in the camps – he and one of his sisters were the only ones to survive. He was a distinguished neurologist and one of the ways he kept his sanity was by observing himself and his fellow prisoners, as if he and they were taking part in a big experiment. After going through phases of shock, disbelief, apathy and hopelessness he saw everything being taken away from himself and*

the other prisoners, everything but one thing which he called the last of the human freedoms – and that was 'to choose one's attitude in any given set of circumstances, to choose one's own way' (Frankl 2004, p. 75). What he found to be critical in those who were able to survive was being able to see that they had still something they wanted to do in their lives. They had a goal or a sense of purpose – a mission in life – something that could not be done by anyone else. From this insight he developed a new school of psychotherapy to help people deal with change across different areas of life.

In a key sense all the conversations have rested ultimately on the belief that a person has awareness and that change is possible. Whatever their genetic or biological inheritance, upbringing or circumstances, a person can be self-determining through their own awareness and choices.

Using PNV Resource 30, emphasise that this applies to those situations where the person may use violence. There is always the possibility of reacting in a way that is not simply the product of nurture or nature but a product of choice (Covey 2004).

The conversation may move on when the person has acknowledged a sense of responsibility for any future decisions in relation to their commitment to non-violence and how this relates to what is important in their life

Element 4 My strengths and staying safe

If the person accepts that they have the power to make positive safe choices in the future, can he or she also identify personal characteristics that will help them in this regard? From previous conversations with the person, you may be able to identify an aspect of their participation (e.g. their thoughtfulness, commitment, openness, determination, etc.) that you could suggest will be relevant to their continuing efforts to stay safe. In the ethos of motivational interviewing it is important that any affirmation should be genuine and real (Miller and Rollnick 2002).

The purpose is not purely about building the person's self-esteem. The focus should always be on the responsibility for the person to make positive change, and the strengths that the person has that may support their efforts. Pinker (2012) argues that violence is rarely a problem of too little self-esteem. He asserts that it is more usual to be associated with too much, especially when it is unearned.

PNV Resource 31 may be used to help stimulate the person to identify some of their own personal strengths. The person may also go further in thinking about possible risk scenarios in the future where there would be a possibility of further violence. Can the person see this coming and begin to connect this with key strengths that may be important in staying non-violent? Hopefully, some new thinking and ways of handling feelings may be among their most relevant strengths.

The conversation may move on when the person has identified at least one personal attribute that may help sustain their efforts towards staying non-violent and has also reflected on how this may help in a possible future situation of risk.

Element 5 Moving towards my positive 'triangle' of behaviour

Ask the person to recall the bus driving past the three people mentioned in Conversation 5. Point out that the bus does not stop because it is full of passengers who have to be at an airport in time to catch a flight. The passengers are noisy and boisterous and have been drinking. They are worried about being late and are shouting out conflicting suggestions and orders about the best and quickest way to get to the airport on time:

> *take next right   no that's too long a way – go straight ahead – go a different way you're driving too slow – we'll never make it – go back – go right – go left, etc.*

However, the bus driver knows exactly where to go and the best and quickest way to get there. Ask the person what the driver should do in relation to all the 'noise' coming from the passengers.

Hopefully the person will agree that what the driver should do is to take no notice of them and just concentrate on driving safely to the airport.

Point out that the person may sometimes have to deal with an unhelpful, noisy din coming from their own thoughts and feelings – a bit like the boisterous passengers on the bus. On such occasions, like the bus driver, the person may just have to keep focused on not resorting to violent acts. Making such difficult choices, despite their thoughts and feelings, may establish positive habits. Sustaining non-violent habits may eventually help the person to also move forward with their thinking and feeling and create a more virtuous circle.

While there would be little point in the bus driver trying to engage with the intoxicated passengers, this should not be the case with the person's unhelpful thoughts and feelings. These should continue to be dealt with as the person has been doing throughout the conversations.

Remind the person of the triangle of behaviour, of thoughts, feelings and actions which they used to consider an example of their past violent behaviour. The person now needs to go forward with a much more positive or 'benign' triangle of behaviour.

The triangle should now be about bringing together more positive actions, thinking and ways of dealing with their feelings that will promote non-violence in the person's life. PNV Resource 32 may be used to record the key steps in each of these three areas that the person has or will continue to take. Some of these will already be clear from the review of the previous conversations in Element 2 above.

Change is multi-faceted and may also involve having to draw from various other sources that can support a person trying to get safer. Other interventions, including counselling, therapy and various recovery programmes, if not already considered, may contribute towards non-violence. Interactions with family, friends, community resources and church may also help people recognise and concentrate, and build on progress. Returning to the assessment of need that should have pre-dated the conversations, the journey towards non-violence has to go forward within the broader context of the person's life. For example, a young person who is trying to move away from gang-related violence may be able to connect to community safety resources to help support and sustain the personal efforts that have been made. Decisions in relation to taking action in any of these areas may also be recorded on the actions point of the positive triangle of behaviour.

PNV Resource 32 also allows consideration to be given to the issue of the person's previous violence and engagement with any of those who have been on the receiving end of the violence. The option of aligning or engaging with appropriate mediation, community or restorative processes may need to be considered, and this should be done within an agreed risk management plan (see Appendix 2).

The conversation may move on to its final element when the person has completed their positive triangle in terms of better actions, thinking and dealing with feeling that may help towards non-violence.

Element 6 Is the wall down and will it stay down?

Particularly if the person's involvement in the conversations has been part of a broader intervention, a report on the outcomes may need to be agreed. The person's participation and attendance can be commented on but its essence should be a summary of the person's stated learning outcomes in relation to each of the conversations, and this may already have been partially completed in Element 2 above.

In moving towards closure, I usually refer to my own experiences of change throughout my life. I mention that I have lived with some wounds, bad habits and temperamental flaws over the years – some of these long-standing and pretty ingrained. Even if I am aware of some of these, I have not always found it that easy to do something about them. I affirm the person for their efforts to address difficult issues within their own life.

I also make the point that while I have done my best to listen to and understand the traumas and adversities the person has experienced in her or his life, I may well not have been able to fully appreciate these. I do this respectfully to acknowledge that only the person will really know the challenges they have had to face in their life.

Confirm that the work is done – a final comment from the person as to how they are feeling and then a cup of tea or coffee.

(PNV Resource 33 is provided for taking some feedback from the person as to how they have found the conversations. The person may agree to do this at this or some later point.)

Notes

1. Figures taken from a report prepared by the Northern Ireland Community Relations Council in 2016. Furthermore, at the time of writing some of my colleagues within the Northern Ireland Probation Service have been subject to threats from a paramilitary group.
2. Vaclac Havel was the first president of the Czech Republic, Human Rights champion and intellectual who made this remark at a Fourth of July speech in Philadelphia in 1994. In a sense, it sums up the essence of the work the person has been doing in striving for greater awareness of what is important and key to their life and how to go forward without violence. His speech also revisits the first conversation when the importance of the person's deep inner life in terms of their mental, emotional and spiritual essence was explored.

References

Bean, K. (2007) *The New Politics of Sinn Féin*. Liverpool: Liverpool University Press.
Covey, S. (2004) *The 8th Habit: From Effectiveness to Greatness*. London: Simon & Schuster.
Frankl, V. (2004) *Man's Search for Meaning*. London: Rider.
Miller, R.W. and Rollnick, S. (2002) *Motivational Interviewing Preparing People for Change*. London: The Guilford Press.
Pinker, S. (2012) *The Better Angels of Our Nature*. London: Penguin.

Conclusion

The Northern Ireland Peace Process and non-violence

John Hume, in a powerful speech at his Nobel Peace prize ceremony on 10 December 1998, talked about the Northern Ireland Peace Process as a rebuke to the evil that violence represents, to the carnage and waste of violence, to its ultimate futility. The process he instigated was supported by a collection of brave women and men. In its ensuing manifestations in the Good Friday (Belfast) Agreement and subsequent negotiations and processes, all rejected violence and sought to make progress based on the principles of 'partnership, equality, and mutual respect'. In particular, John Hume sought to promote his message of peace and non-violence through conversations with anyone who would listen. 'I say it and go on saying it until I hear the man in the pub saying my words back to me' (Hume in Routledge 1997, p. 5).

Common violence and professional social work practice

Similarly with common violence. Dialogue with those using violence should be at the forefront of social work practice.

Social work engagement will always strive for a clear and comprehensive idea of a person's needs and situation. This is not a technical job; it is a human job. It is often complicated, nuanced and unpredictable, and needs to be related to the contingencies of each situation. It is about creating a relationship with another human being in order to help them. This includes offering a person the opportunity, time and engagement to consider moving towards non-violence.

There has been a growing industry of 'specialist' interventions across many areas of violence, some of which make helpful contributions. However, care needs to be taken not just to throw people into programmes in the belief we can treat them out of something for which there may be a range of diverse elements playing out, some of which may well be to do with adversities and inequalities in a person's life. Social work always has to balance the psychology with the sociology, keeping both grounded in its core values.

Referrals to such programmes should be decided within the overall comprehensive risk assessment of the situation. They do not remove the responsibility on social work to engage with violence, nor should they undermine the belief and confidence that it can do so effectively. There are common causes and cross-cutting risk factors across the different types of common violence which can be addressed by social workers (WHO 2004). This publication, and the conversations contained within it, has been offered as a contribution to helping all social workers take such practice forward and to continue to learn and build professional capacity.

The organisational culture

Positive social work practice promoting non-violence will rely on the systems and the culture at play within the organisations in which it takes place. Taking forward the relationship-based and person-centred ethos at the heart of the conversations always needs to be balanced with realism in terms of the risks that the person being worked with presents to others and how these should be addressed. An overview of serious case reviews in Northern Ireland highlighted the 'need for regular and sufficiently frequent supervision that challenges and allows for reflection' (Devaney et al. 2013, p. 56). I was fortunate, most of the time, to experience supervision in which I was able to talk openly about my anxieties and fears in dealing with those who used violence and continue to be helped to 'police my own biases'. Furthermore, vulnerability was not seen as a sign of weakness or incompetence but rather as showing emotional intelligence and strength (Wonnacott 2012).

The organisational culture should be one that has high expectations, provides unflagging support, recognises the importance of reflective supervision and strives to avoid an overly procedural and fear-dominated ethos. By doing so, it will, in a real sense, be modelling the critical messages contained within each of the conversations in the dialogue between the social worker and the person working towards non-violence.

Moving forward

Common violence is endemic; it goes across a fluid continuum of risk and much of it will not go into a formal justice system. All common violence, however low level, impacts upon someone's quality of life and community safety, and has consequences (Wolf 2007). Nelson Mandela, in the same speech referred to in the introduction in which he spoke about common violence, also challenged the assumption that violence is an intrinsic part of the human condition (Mandela 2002). Violence always needs to be engaged with. It can be transformed. This publication asserts social work's responsibility to seek to do so and to continue to promote non-violence. This is the essence of social work in striving to sustain and empower people to live safely within their relationships, families and communities.

References

Devaney, J., Bunting, L., Hayes, D. and Lazenbatt, A. (2013) *Translating Learning into Action: An Overview of Learning Arising from Case Management Reviews in Northern Ireland 2003–2008*. Belfast: DHSSPS, QUB & NSPCC.

Mandela, N. (2002) *Introduction to World Report on Violence and Health*. Geneva: WHO.

Routledge, P. (1997) *John Hume: A Biography*. London: HarperCollins.

Wolf, R.V. (2007) *Principles of Problem Solving Justice*. New York: Bureau of Justice Assistance.

Wonnacott, J. (2012) *Mastering Social Work Supervision*. London: Jessica Kingsley.

World Health Organisation (2004) *Preventing Violence: A Guide to Implementing the Recommendations of the World Report on Violence and Health*. Geneva: WHO.

Appendix 1

Resource sheets

The Resources are related to specific elements within each of the conversations and are addressed directly to the person.

They may be used for individual work with people and photocopied for this purpose.

They may be retained by the person for further reflection or working between meetings, or as a reminder of work completed.

PNV Resource 1 My daily reflection

How serious a problem has my use of violent actions been today:

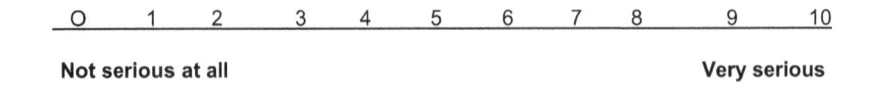

```
 0   1   2   3   4   5   6   7   8   9   10
```
Not serious at all   **Very serious**

If serious – why was this so?

Was I involved in any conflicts today?   Yes/No

If yes, how did I deal with them?

What were my thoughts and feelings when violence was a problem today?

Was I in a situation where I felt provoked, embarrassed, shamed, angered, annoyed, etc. and I could have been aggressive or violent, but chose not to be?

What did I think, feel or do that helped me stay non-violent and safe?

Remember: I will only learn by doing!

Appendix 1   131

PNV Resource 2 How serious a problem is my use of violent behaviour for me?

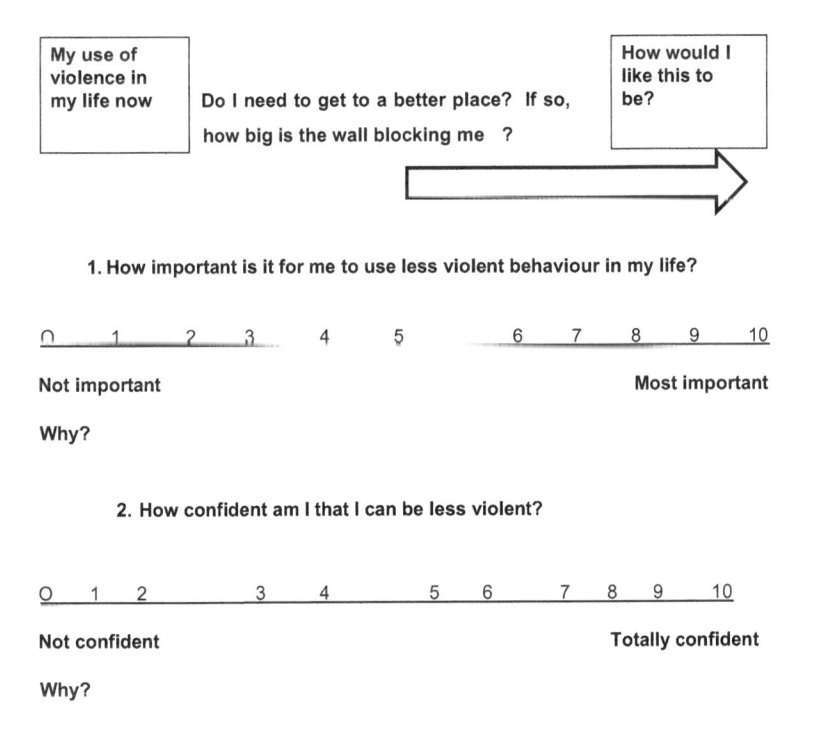

My use of violence in my life now	Do I need to get to a better place? If so, how big is the wall blocking me ?	How would I like this to be?

1. How important is it for me to use less violent behaviour in my life?

0   1   2   3   4   5   6   7   8   9   10

Not important   Most important

Why?

2. How confident am I that I can be less violent?

0   1   2   3   4   5   6   7   8   9   10

Not confident   Totally confident

Why?

I need to bring down the wall blocking my path to non-violence!

PNV Resource 3 The cycle of change

First, think about an example from another area of life (e.g. smoking, drinking, diet, exercise, etc.) where you, or someone you know, have tried or have succeeded in making significant change. Start with the 'Not thinking about change' circle.

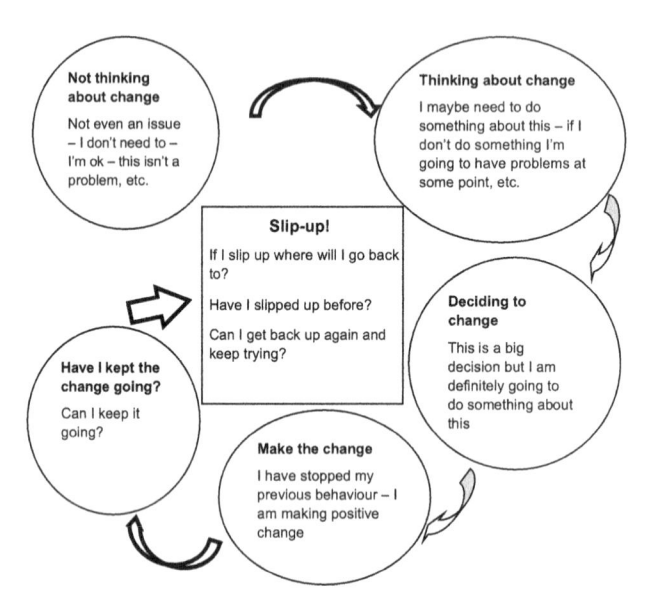

Not thinking about change
Not even an issue – I don't need to – I'm ok – this isn't a problem, etc.

Thinking about change
I maybe need to do something about this – if I don't do something I'm going to have problems at some point, etc.

Deciding to change
This is a big decision but I am definitely going to do something about this

Make the change
I have stopped my previous behaviour – I am making positive change

Have I kept the change going?
Can I keep it going?

Slip-up!
If I slip up where will I go back to?
Have I slipped up before?
Can I get back up again and keep trying?

With regard to my use of violence, how ready, willing and able am I to change?

In which of the above circles would I currently put myself?

How many times have I been in this process before and slipped back?

Nobody succeeds the first-time round but it may bring us closer to change!

PNV Resource 4 Important personal goal(s), life balance and non-violence

How do I want my life to be in three years' time?

What are my very important personal goals?

1
2
3

MY LIFE BALANCE AND MY GOALS?

> **PHYSICAL** (Body)
>
> Healthy living and looking after myself – my physical and mental health? How is my diet? Do I have to work long hours? Do I have enough to live on? How is my sleep? Addiction issues? Stress?

> **MENTAL** (Mind)
>
> Continuing to open myself to new learning and increasing my knowledge.
>
> Am I bringing unsuitable violence-related material or pornography into my mind?

> **EMOTIONAL** (Heart)
>
> Having healthy friendships, relationships and social life – caring and supporting others?
>
> Am I putting pressure on these by any aspect of my lifestyle?

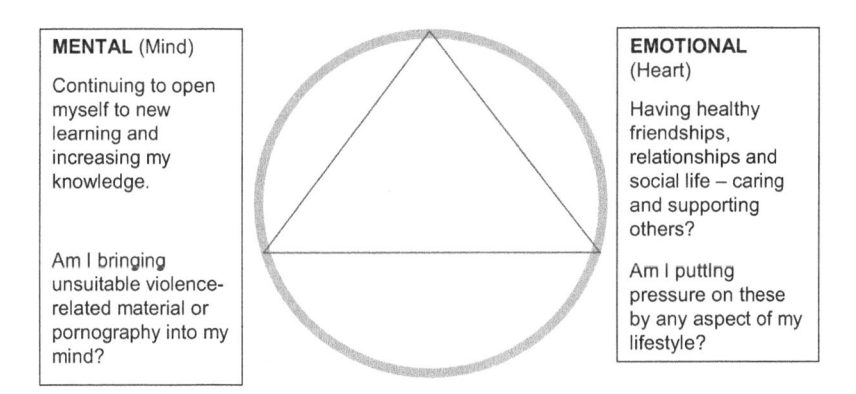

Does the circle mean anything for me?

(Something greater outside of myself that gives inner peace and helps me to be safer?)

Things that are important to me can shape my behaviour.

PNV Resource 5 Thinking about and understanding violence

1   How do my '12 words' compare with the statement below?

Any behaviour by an individual that intentionally threatens or causes physical, sexual or psychological harm to others or to themselves.

Consider the following five examples of violence:

i. Paul and some friends chase another young man down the street and start punching and kicking him, calling him a 'Syrian refugee bastard'.

ii. Pete, aged 19, has been arguing with his girlfriend. He suddenly stands over her and stares hard at her. She knows immediately to be quiet.

iii. Mark, aged 17, makes a sexual comment online about Anne, aged 14, which distresses her.

iv. Jo is always criticising Jackie's family and friends and that Jackie should have nothing to do with them, as they are really bad news and Jackie is as bad as they are. It should just be about the two of them if they really love each other.

v. Mary, aged 50, cares for her elderly mother. Her mother has made a mess in the kitchen while preparing dinner. Mary looks scornfully at her: 'You really are a dirty old woman, you'd be better off dead and stop ruining my life.'

2   What types of violence are described above?

physical – threatening – sexual – controlling – emotional ?

3   Five other specific actions for each of the above types of violence.

4   How common are the five types of violence?

5   Who carries out such acts of violence?

Violence is about using power to harm.

PNV Resource 6 My use of violent actions?

PHYSICAL: *'Assaulting'*

Hitting, slapping, punching, pushing and shoving, pulling hair, pulling and grabbing, twisting arms, choking, kicking, biting, stabbing, using objects and weapons, etc.

THREATENING: *The 'tightrope'*

Making verbal threats, shouting and screaming, standing over someone, swearing, staring, pointing, damaging possessions, throwing things, driving recklessly, pretending to be about to hit someone, getting in a person's face, stalking, etc.

SEXUAL: *The 'object'*

Pressurising someone into unwanted sexual behaviour, forcing someone to use pornography, sexualised talk, ridiculing someone's appearance, grooming, affairs, sexual abuse on social media, etc.

CONTROLLING: *Bossing*

Always knowing better, telling someone what to do, controlling money, making all the decisions, isolating, humiliating a person in front of others, criticising a person's family or friends, checking up, questioning, deciding what someone wears, etc.

EMOTIONAL/PSYCHOLOGICAL: *The put-down*

Name calling, criticising, fault finding, blaming, disrespecting, playing mind games, making a person feel guilty, not listening, not respecting feelings, trying to provoke arguments, dramatic mood swings, denying, manipulating others against the person, etc.

1. What types of the above violent actions do I tend to use and with whom?

2. Do my actions happen: **Rarely**   **Sometimes**   **Often**   **Regularly**

3. Are my actions

   Not at all serious   Extremely serious
   0   1   2   3   4   5   6   7   8   9   10

4. How is power connected with my use of violent actions?

136 Appendix 1

PNV Resource 7 An example of violent behaviour: more than just actions!

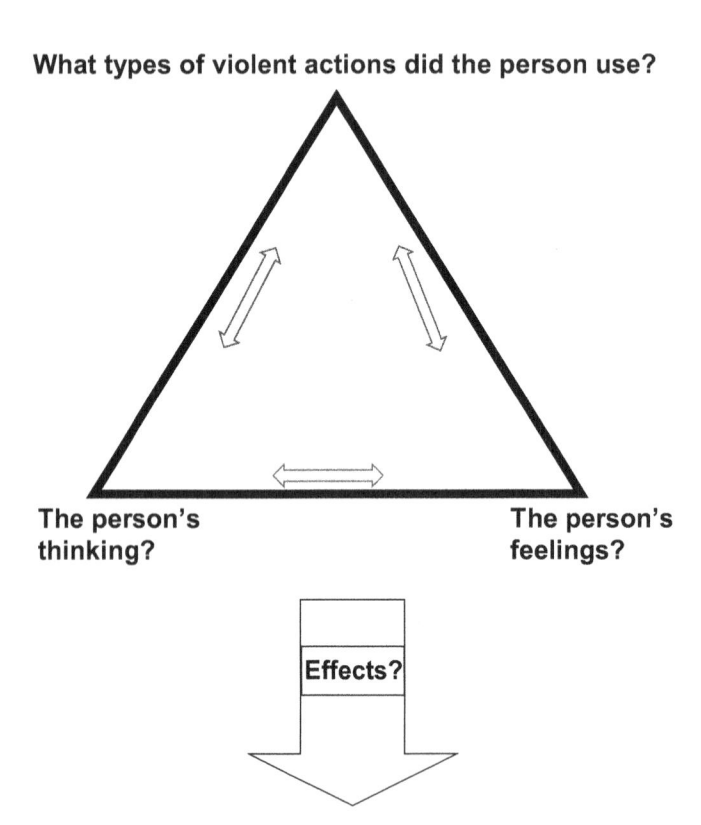

What types of violent actions did the person use?

The person's thinking?

The person's feelings?

Effects?

Now can you think of at least one way that the person who was violent could have thought, or felt, or acted, that might have been safer and perhaps helped avoid the use of violent acts?

PNV Resource 8 Linking an example of my violent acts to my thinking and feelings

What was the situation leading up to my use of violence?

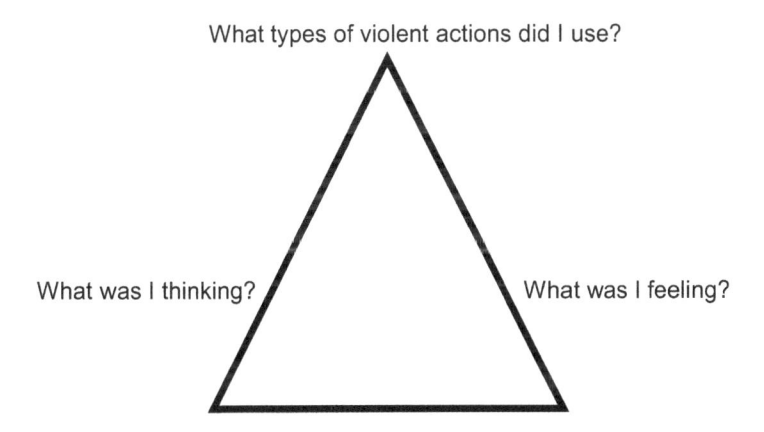

What types of violent actions did I use?

What was I thinking?   What was I feeling?

What did I immediately gain from my violent acts?

Can I identify a new or different thought, or way of handling my feelings, or a different action that may have kept me safer?

PNV Resource 9: My encounters with violence

What happened to me?

> What are my first memories of violence within my family of origin, my school, my community?

> As I moved through my teenage years, what were my experiences of violence?

Did others ever abuse their power against me?
Physically? – Emotionally? – Sexually?   **NOW**

BIRTH

> How were conflicts dealt with?

> When did violence become something I could choose to use? What made it the best choice?
>
> In what ways was it positive?
>
> Was it ever stronger than me – or was I the stronger?

What happens in the future often depends on what has happened in the past.

PNV Resource 10 Being a man?

Am I doing the right thing, in the right way, for the right reason?

Controlling	Handling power safely
Aggressive	Assertive
Over-confident, tough	Vulnerable
Keep proving myself	Accepting
Arrogant/always right	Humility
Not committed/Uncaring	Commitment
Abusive	Respectful
Dishonourable	Honourable
Irresponsible	Responsible
Not showing feelings	Open about feelings

Think about the relationship(s) in which my use of violence has happened.

Where am I on the lines and where do I need to get to, to be non-violent?

PNV Resource 11 Power issues and my use of violence

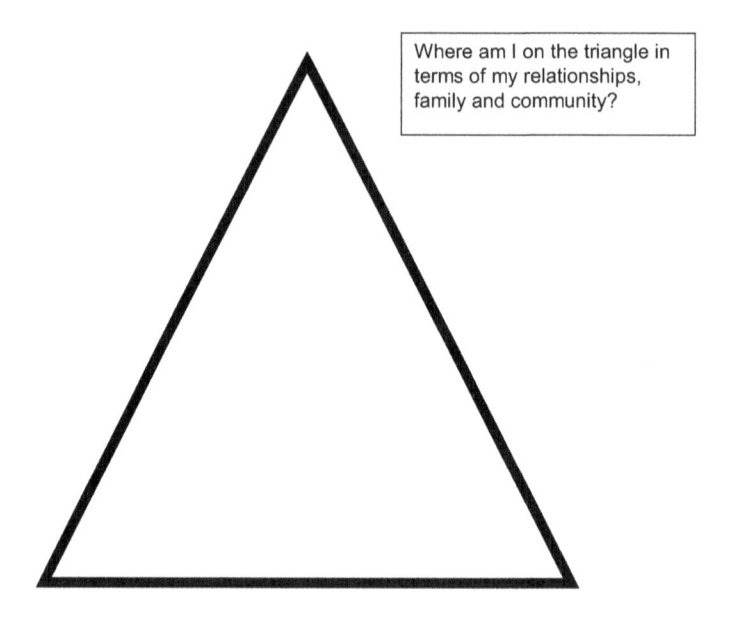

> Where am I on the triangle in terms of my relationships, family and community?

1. Where am I and my victim(s) and other witnesses on the triangle?
2. Was the 'victim' of my violence someone who was clearly powerless or maybe it was someone who actually had or I thought had more power?
3. In what ways did I feel I was not getting what I expected or wanted?
4. What was my sense of entitlement behind the violence?
5. Was I worried or angry that what should have been provided was not?
6. How did I realise that I was not going to get what I wanted or felt entitled to?
7. Can I understand the hurt emotions and see at least some aspects of my violence as thoughtful, deliberate, intentional and about getting some power?
8. Was my violence indirectly linked to other areas of my life where I felt totally powerless and this allowed me to get some sense of dominance and control?

PNV Resource 12 How is violence impacting upon my life now?

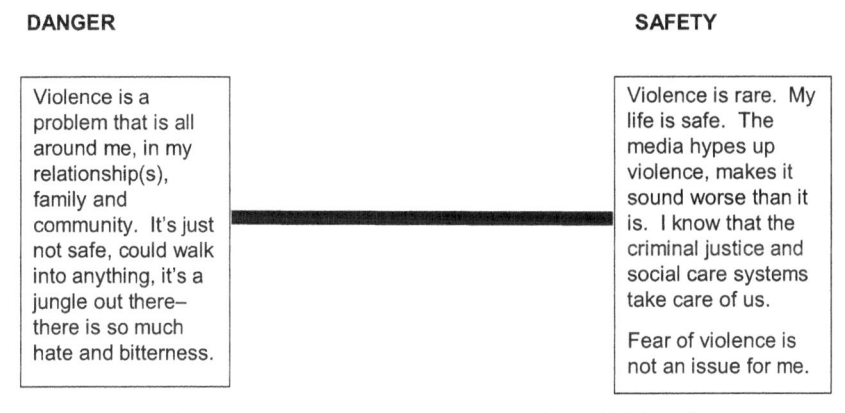

DANGER   **SAFETY**

| Violence is a problem that is all around me, in my relationship(s), family and community. It's just not safe, could walk into anything, it's a jungle out there– there is so much hate and bitterness. | ———————— | Violence is rare. My life is safe. The media hypes up violence, makes it sound worse than it is. I know that the criminal justice and social care systems take care of us.

Fear of violence is not an issue for me. |

Where am I on the line? Does my position change if I am thinking about my relationship or my family or the community?

How much control does violence have over me?

0   1   2   3   4   5   6   7   8   9   10

No control   Total control

What does the violence want me to become?

Violence is the problem, not me!

If I was thinking about the risk of violence coming from myself – where am I on the continuum of risk?

How safe am I to others?

Why am I safe to others?

PNV Resource 13 The effects of violence

Each experience of violence will affect each individual in different ways and needs to be considered carefully and sensitively.

Physical harm?

Bruising – cuts – fractures – black eyes – lost teeth – broken nose – lost hair – burns – stab wounds – multiple injuries – disability – others?

Psychological and emotional harm?

Shock – fear – terror – anger – uncertainty – confusion – humiliation – embarrassment – guilt – shame – betrayal – disgust – put down – used – violation – anxiety – insecure – resentful – ambivalent – helpless – degraded – 'dirty' – belittled – worthless – others?

Behavioural harm?

Being on edge – withdrawn – not going out as much – isolation from family and friends – revengeful – resorting to alcohol or drugs – distrusting people – poor mental health – poor self-care and loss of self-respect – risk-taking behaviour – self-harming – thoughts about suicide – apathy and couldn't care less – apathetic – depressed – damaged relationships – loss of sexual feelings – flat – withdrawn – behaving differently – anxious – clingy – aggressive – problems sleeping – eating disorders – wetting the bed – soiled clothes – take risks – absence from school – changes in eating habits – obsessive behaviour – nightmares – flashbacks – self-harm – loss of sense of identity – poor educational outcomes.

> **Explore:**
> - Experiencing **FEAR AND ANGER** at the same time?
> - Experiencing **UNCERTAINTY** after the violence – expecting more?
> - Experiencing ongoing **PATTERN** of violence?
> - Experiencing a lot of mixed and confused feelings?
> - Short-term or long-term effects?
> - Survival and recovery?

PNV Resource 14 A cycle of violence? (Adapted from Walker 1979)

Frankie and Pat have been in a relationship for three years. Following explosive outbursts from Frankie, involving yelling, put-downs, pushes and shoves, etc., the couple go through the following cycle:

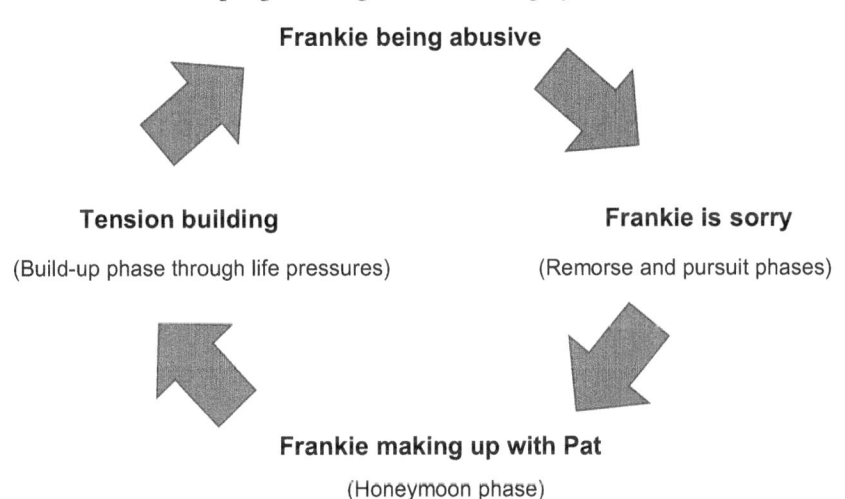

Frankie being abusive

Tension building

(Build-up phase through life pressures)

Frankie is sorry

(Remorse and pursuit phases)

Frankie making up with Pat

(Honeymoon phase)

- If Frankie keeps being abusive to Pat how meaningful are the apologies?
- How might Pat begin to see and feel about these apologies and the making up?
- Could they become more about Frankie wanting sex and Pat feeling degraded?
- Will Pat begin to feel the tension-building phase more like 'fault finding' and walking on eggshells, full of anxiety and uncertainty, and just waiting for the next explosion?
- How might Pat deal with such tension – to bring it to a head and get it over with?
- Might Frankie then start to blame Pat for these incidents rather than apologising?
- How will power and authority and entitlement issues play out?
- What will be the long-term impact of all this upon their relationship?
- How does my example of violence fit within a bigger pattern or cycle of control?

144 Appendix 1

PNV Resource 15 Children's development and violence

All children need to be protected from serious trauma and chronic stress and to be provided with secure, nurturing relationships with parents within a safe community.

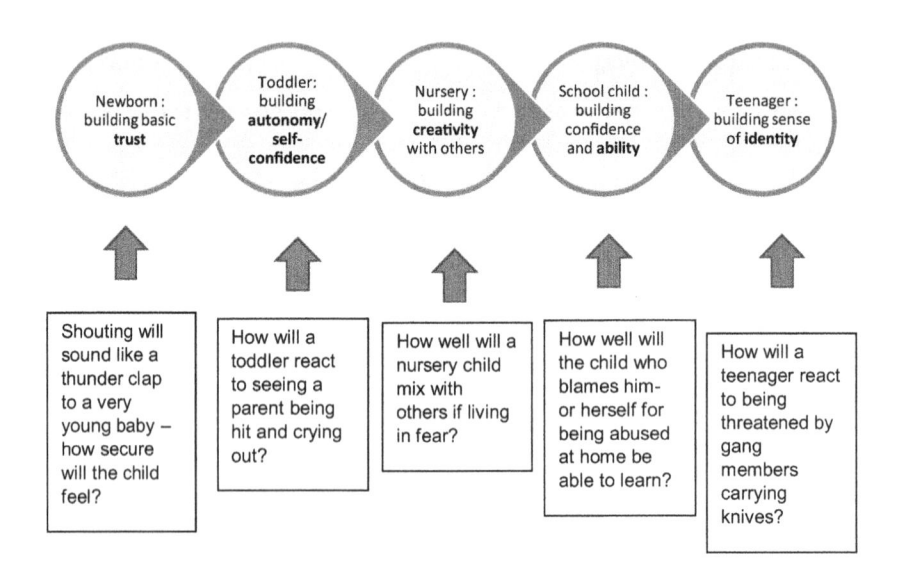

Newborn: building basic **trust** → Toddler: building **autonomy/self-confidence** → Nursery: building **creativity** with others → School child: building confidence and **ability** → Teenager: building sense of **identity**

- Shouting will sound like a thunder clap to a very young baby – how secure will the child feel?
- How will a toddler react to seeing a parent being hit and crying out?
- How well will a nursery child mix with others if living in fear?
- How well will the child who blames him- or herself for being abused at home be able to learn?
- How will a teenager react to being threatened by gang members carrying knives?

Exposure to violence by a child as a victim or as a witness may lead to health-harming effects throughout their life.

- How has any child or young person been affected by or caught up in or witnessed any of the violence I have used?
- How might this have impacted upon the child(ren) or young person(s)?
- In what ways may my violence have affected the different and vital stages of their development?

PNV Resource 16 Taking responsibility and trying to clear up my mess

I have accepted that some of my actions have been violent. I have also used some of the following 'excuses' rather than take responsibility for my actions. [.]

I just snapped – I didn't do anything wrong – I don't remember – I didn't mean to hurt you – I was acting in self-defence – I'm not really violent – You're making it up – That's how people behave where I come from – I was only trying to hold you – I hardly touched you – You're exaggerating – I was under a lot of pressure – I only threw something at you to get you to shut up – You bruise easily – It wasn't that bad – I was drunk – You pushed me too far – That's how my father/mother treated my mother/father – I just lost control – You provoked me – I did it to get you to do what you were told – You made me jealous – You hit me first – I have a bad temper I can't control – You know I won't really hurt you.

I can go further and show my understanding of the impact of my use of violence on the person by describing the harm I caused in the person's own words. [.]

Doing this work shows how important being non-violent is to me.
My violence has caused harm. In trying to sort it out my position on the line is:

Quick fixes   Longterm solutions

It may never be possible to reach a full solution for the harm I have done. What do I need to do to keep moving towards taking responsibility and clearing up the mess?

PNV Resource 17 Connecting thinking and violence

Record again below some of the examples of thinking that were related to the acts of violence discussed in Conversation 2 (revisit Resources 7 and 8).

Was any of my thinking similar to the ways of thinking below that research has also identified as related to violent acts?

- Thinking I should be entitled to get what I want/need from others.

- Thinking I am better than/superior to others.

- Thinking that other people are hostile or against me or can't be trusted.

- Thinking that certain people are worthless or worse.

- Thinking I should have something right away.

- Thinking I should be in control.

- Thinking I shouldn't have to put up with annoyance or frustration.

- Thinking I should be always treated with respect.

PNV Resource 18 Punching holes in my thinking and new thinking

Returning to the example of my violence in PNV Resource 8 can I get a clearer idea of my thinking 'map'?

PART 1

i. What were the **justifications** in my own mind for my violent actions?

ii. Why did I have the **ability** to be violent in the way I was at the time? How comfortable was I in doing what I did?

iii. How did I weigh up the **consequences** of deciding to be violent? What did I think it might lead to?

iv. What **alternatives** did I consider and why did I not choose any of these?

PART 2

Which ways of thinking do I need to try to move away from?

New thinking that might help me bring the wall down and continue moving towards non-violence?

PNV Resource 19 More safer thinking

As well as the changes in my thinking I have already identified I have picked out more positive thoughts (see below). Thinking in these ways may help me to be safer:

- I can accept and like myself.
- I can control what I do and not do to other people.
- I can accept criticism.
- I can accept that I am not right all the time.
- I can feel that it is ok to walk away from a fight.
- I can hear other people's anger and not feel threatened or get angry back.
- It's ok to feel insecure and uncertain at times.
- I don't need everyone to like me.
- I don't have to rise to the bait when I think other people are trying to wind me up.
- I don't have to feel I'm the centre of attention to feel good.
- It's ok to feel scared about things at times: life can be scary.
- I am not entitled to expect people to behave in ways I want them to behave.

PNV Resource 20 Emotions and feelings

How aware am I of my emotions? How many of these were on my list?

joy – love – happy – pleased – calm – relaxed – contented – stimulated – enthusiastic – peaceful – relaxed – confident – spontaneous – accepting – alert – passionate – excited – close – determined – secure – proud – inspired – respected

sadness – upset – let down – anxious – disappointed – depressed – low – frustrated – regretful – confused – tense – embarrassed – lonely

angry – annoyed – frustrated – outraged – furious – rage – contempt – hate

fear – frightened – terrified – abandoned – jealous

disgusted – mixed up – dislike – bored –

guilt – shame – humiliated

Emotions

- like our fingerprints, everyone has them but we feel them in unique ways, they are ours, we own them;
- neither good nor bad, right or wrong, they simply are;
- we feel emotions in our bodies – not thoughts or facts – may carry important messages worth listening to;
- often associated with other people and our relationships;
- can be sources of energy and power or they can take away our energy;
- we bury our emotions alive, and they will find some way of coming back;
- stay in touch with and feel our feelings but separate them from instant action.

Which emotions do I find most difficult to be open about?

Which emotions may be related to my use of violence?

150   Appendix 1

PNV Resource 21 Anger and my use of violence

How often do I go through the stages of anger shown below?

4. CRISIS POINT

The point at which I behaved in a physically or verbally or emotionally abusive way. I was out of control. I blew my top. I lost it. My body was flooded and pumped up with high levels of stress chemicals and blood pressure. How dangerous was I?

3. Moving up

The exhilarating and energising process in getting myself worked up with self-righteous inner talk giving me convincing arguments for venting anger. Adrenalin now starting to pump through my body. Why could I not step away or think differently about the situation?

5. Recovery

How did I come back down and deal with the adrenalin that remained in my system for approximately 90 minutes? Did I shoot back up again?

2. Triggers

What specifically pushed my button and got me going?

What does this say about my expectations and the way I think?

1. Baseline

How am I normally – easygoing, laid back or much quicker to fly off the handle and more on edge, etc.

What was my situation at the time I am thinking about?

6. The dip

Regret, depression, feeling sorry for myself? Did I try to make up?

Not easy to talk myself out of something I've behaved myself into!

Remember: anger is as natural as being thirsty!
Venting anger or suppressing it can be harmful.
Can I let off some steam and not act on my anger too much?

PNV Resource 22 Emotions and my use of violence

> 1   In the example of my use of violence I was experiencing the following emotions:

Do I accept that these emotions which I was experiencing in my own unique way have also been felt by literally billions of people, and there is nothing uniquely wrong with me, that they are part of being human?

> 2   My advice to myself now in how to better manage the above emotions, as if it was being given to me by a wise and experienced person, is that [.]

3   To what degree do the roots of my violence lie in my feelings and thinking coming together to create a sense of entitlement and having power? What key messages do I need to take forward to manage my thinking and emotions better so as to be safer?

   1.

   2.

   3.

Can I bring my thoughts and feelings together to achieve a better balance?

PNV Resource 23(i) Some ideas to help my 'emotional intelligence'

Dealing with challenging situations which have stirred my emotions can be difficult.

Can I remember that the most important thing may be to not deal immediately with the problem? Can I try to gain some sense of awareness of my emotions first before then deciding how to deal with the issue provoking me?

Can I slow down and feel my emotions? I don't have to immediately justify or rationalise them. Nor do I have to distract myself or get busy. Can I accept if I am anxious or angry? Can I ask myself what I am feeling right now?

Can I recognise the stress of not dealing with the negative feelings I am experiencing and the danger of them building up? Can I try not to rationalise them and allow them out of my head and into my heart?

Is there anyone I can trust to talk to about my feelings – if I'm flooded or even experiencing new emotions?

Can I keep observing my own reactions to other people – both what I am feeling and thinking inside and also what I show on the outside?

Can I keep trying to do my daily reflection and be a witness to my own reactions as they come up? For example, when someone cuts in front of me while driving, doesn't let me out, criticises me, argues with me, doesn't do what I want, etc.?

The more I feel my own feelings will help me get a sense of where they are coming from and how they may relate to my thinking.

Can I learn over time to bring my thinking and feelings together in a better balance?

Appendix I   153

PNV Resource 23(ii) Further ideas that may help my emotional well-being

An 'emergency relaxation' exercise

For situations in which I am feeling frustrated, annoyed, angry, and could get really worked up and possibly become violent.

- Make sure my body is in an upright position, either sitting or standing (deliberately sit down if possible – a safer position to be in).

- Mentally say 'stop' to myself over and over again, or use another word if preferred (e.g. calm, peace, settle).

- Close my eyes, close my mouth and breathe in deeply through the nostrils. Breathe out slowly through the nostrils.

- Allow my shoulders to drop and the hands to relax. If standing, allow the arms and hands to hang loose. If sitting, allow the arms to slightly bend and the backs of the hands to rest on the thighs.

- Allow the teeth to slightly part, the tongue to rest on the base of the mouth and the jaw to relax.

- Breathe in deeply through the nostrils. Breathe out slowly through the nostrils. Do at least five inhalations and five exhalations.

- Allow breathing to return to normal, letting it find its own speed, length, depth and rhythm.

A 'calmness' moment

Just for a few minutes – be still, notice my frantic thoughts and feelings, relax my shoulders, become aware of my breathing – calm my heart, my mind and my body – just be still.

I can practise this at home for five to ten minutes at any time.

PNV Resource 24 Responding in a 'conflict'

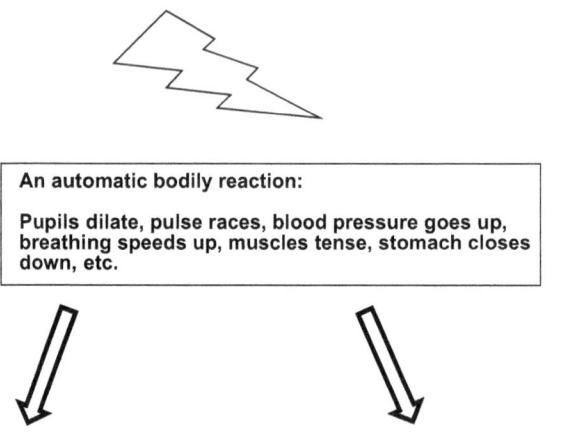

> An automatic bodily reaction:
>
> Pupils dilate, pulse races, blood pressure goes up, breathing speeds up, muscles tense, stomach closes down, etc.

Aggressively (I win/you lose)   **Passively (You win/I lose)**

> What will happen if I always fight and be aggressive?

> What will happen if I always back down and be passive?

If I react differently depending on the nature of the conflict what does this depend on?

Does it always have to be about winning or losing?

Can it ever be a WIN–WIN?

PNV Resource 25 Character contests and loss of face

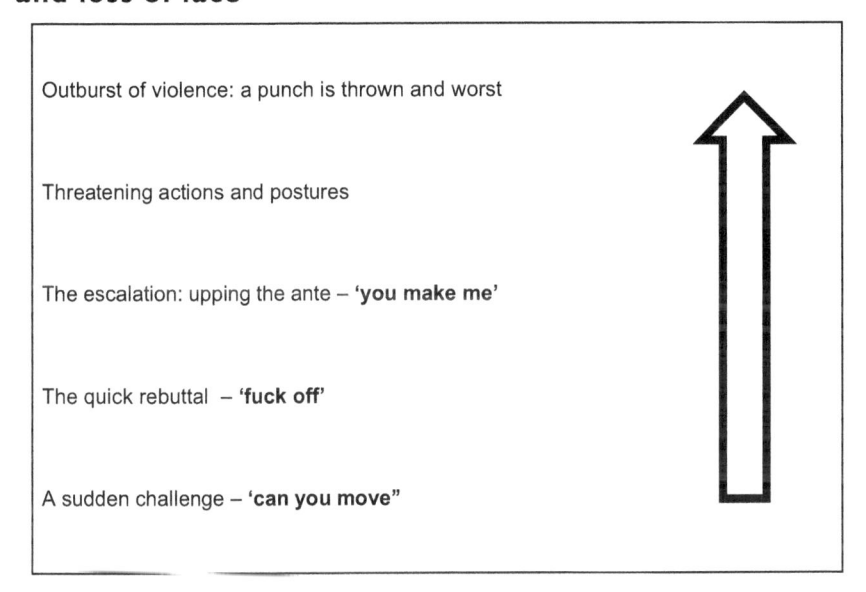

Outburst of violence: a punch is thrown and worst

Threatening actions and postures

The escalation: upping the ante – **'you make me'**

The quick rebuttal – **'fuck off'**

A sudden challenge – **'can you move"**

Attack others
Do I lash out verbally and physcially, turn the tables, blame the victim?

Withdraw:
Do I isolate myself, run and hide?

Shame and loss of face

Avoid:
Do I deny, abuse drugs/alcoho seek thrills ?

Attack self
Do I put myself down?

The Compass of Shame – when I lose face what do I tend to do?

PNV Resource 26 Responding in a conflict

Consider the following conflict between Pat and Frankie. Pat is the parent and Frankie is a 16-year-old young person. The reason Pat is objecting to Frankie going out is that (s)he has just found out that young people have been taking drugs at the venue and also that a young person was stabbed there recently, and Pat is worried about Frankie going there. The conflict erupts as follows:

> **PAT:** You're not going out to that place tonight – no way.
>
> **FRANKIE**: What are you talking about? I told you I'm going and you said it was fine.
>
> **PAT:** Look, I'm not going to say it again, you're not going.
>
> **FRANKIE:** You told me you had no problem with it the other day – I've arranged it with my friend so I'm going.
>
> **PAT**: You're not going and that's the end of it.
>
> **FRANKIE**: You promised you would let me go. You're always lying! I can't believe a single word you say, you hate my friends and you don't trust me, I'm old enough to go. You know I won't do anything stupid or anything, you don't let me do anything I enjoy. You're always messing things up. I hate you and I'm going anyway, I don't fucking care what you say.

If I was Pat the parent, my response would be:

NB: This does not have to be shared.

PNV Resource 27 Five ideas for dealing with conflict

How does my approach in responding to Frankie fit with these five ideas?

1. **The first 90 seconds**
   Would I have been able to manage my reaction in the heat of the moment without going into fight, flight or freeze? How hard would this have been for me?

2. **Trying to listen to and understand the other side's position**
   How well would I have listened and shown I was trying to understand Frankie's thinking and feelings?
   For example: I see you're very annoyed with me, you're mad at me, you don't think I'm being fair, you feel you should be able to go, etc.

3. **Respectfully and clearly communicating my own side**
   Would I have been able to convey my position without attacking or putting down Frankie?
   Did I use any **'I' statements?** For example: I cannot let you go. I believe it's not safe. I have been told there may be trouble. I would never forgive myself if anything happened to you, etc.

4. **Trying to think win/win**
   Would my immediate reaction have pushed me into a win/lose or lose/win? Could I have offered Frankie another option – an alternative night out or positive gesture – trying to get some sort of win/win?

5. **Allowing for the possibility of no agreement**
   Being a parent and protecting my child means I should not give in to Frankie. Would I have been able to hold my ground without giving up on Frankie either?

Appendix 1

PNV Resource 28 My violence, conflict and abusing power

When I consider my example of the use of violence again, can I see its roots within one or more of the circles?

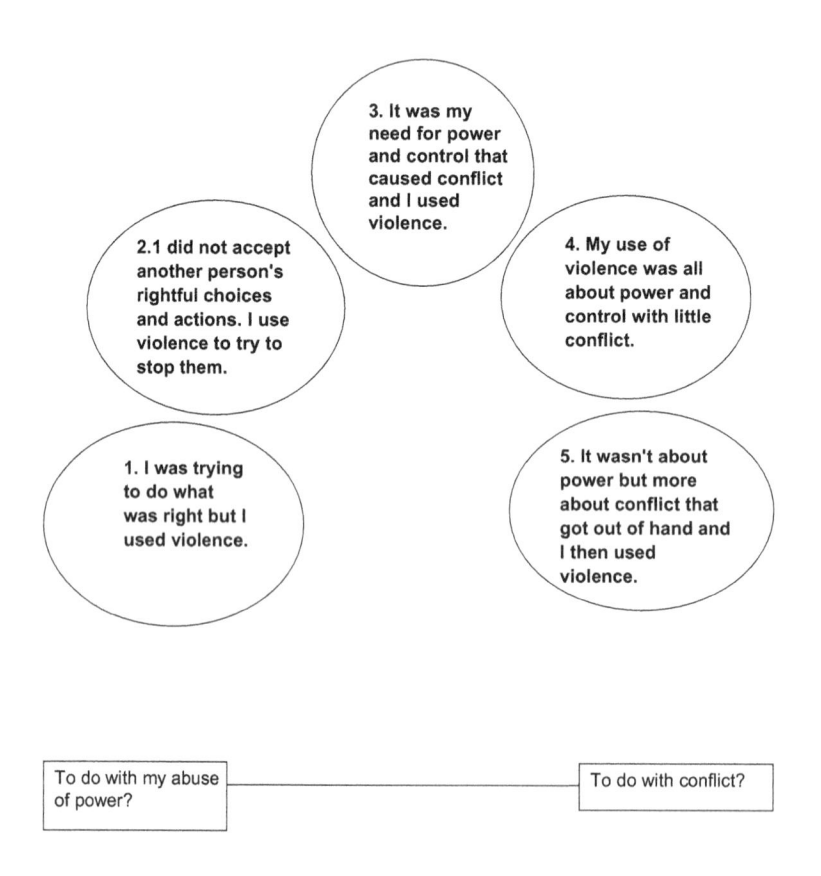

- 3. It was my need for power and control that caused conflict and I used violence.
- 2. I did not accept another person's rightful choices and actions. I use violence to try to stop them.
- 4. My use of violence was all about power and control with little conflict.
- 1. I was trying to do what was right but I used violence.
- 5. It wasn't about power but more about conflict that got out of hand and I then used violence.

| To do with my abuse of power? | ———————————— | To do with conflict? |

Where do my acts of violence mostly sit on the line?

PNV Resource 29 Reviewing my learning

- **Conversation 1: The 'why' question.** My reasons for doing this work and where I am in making positive change towards non-violence and how it fits with my important life goals and balance are:

- **Conversation 2: What is there to talk about?** My understanding of the types and seriousness of violent actions I have used and the thinking and feelings that went with them:

- **Conversation 3: My story and violence.** My past life experiences of violence, my biological sex and power issues and how these relate to my use of violence:

- **Conversation 4: The harm I have caused.** The harm caused to the person(s) at the receiving end of my violence – taking responsibility for the fear, anger and uncertainty – the long-term legacy of my violence:

- **Conversation 5: Punching holes in my thinking towards non-violence.** The negative thinking that is connected with my use of violence and the new positive thinking that will help me stay safer:

- **Conversation 6: Dealing with feeling and non-violence.** The emotions associated with my violence and finding ways of dealing with feelings in moving towards non-violence:

- **Conversation 7: Conflict, power and non-violence.** Being clearer about conflict and not causing it or dealing with it through abuse of my power, and seeking to understand and be understood:

Can I keep on keeping on towards non-violence?

PNV Resource 30 My awareness and the power to choose

I have the gift to step outside my internal world and look in and see if I need to make any changes to how I **think** about things and how I deal with how I **feel**.

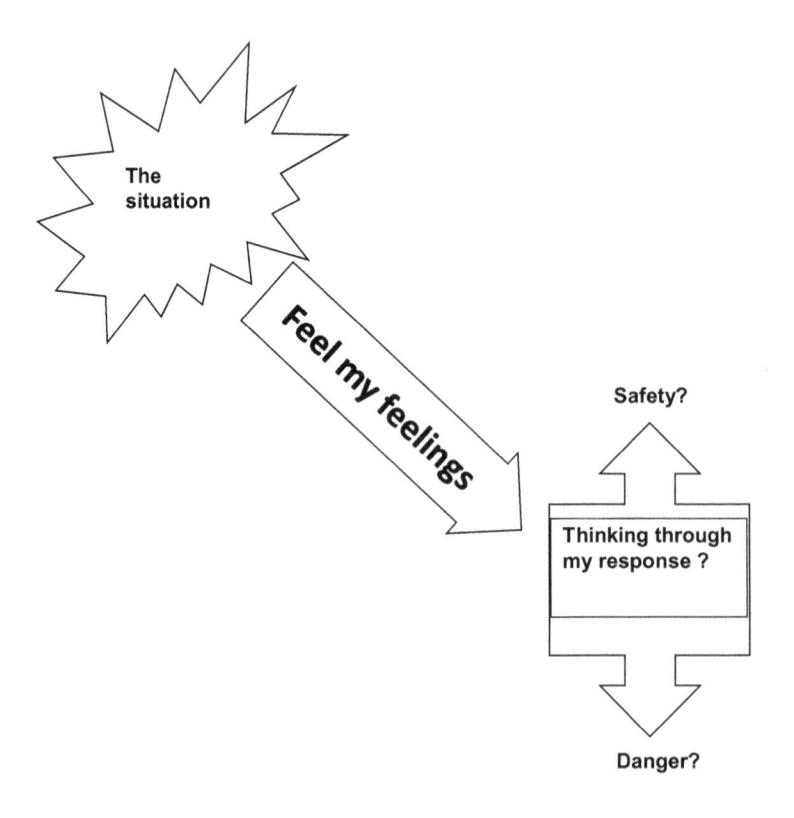

The situation

Feel my feelings

Safety?

Thinking through my response ?

Danger?

If it is to be it is up to me!

Appendix 1

PNV Resource 31 My strengths and staying safe

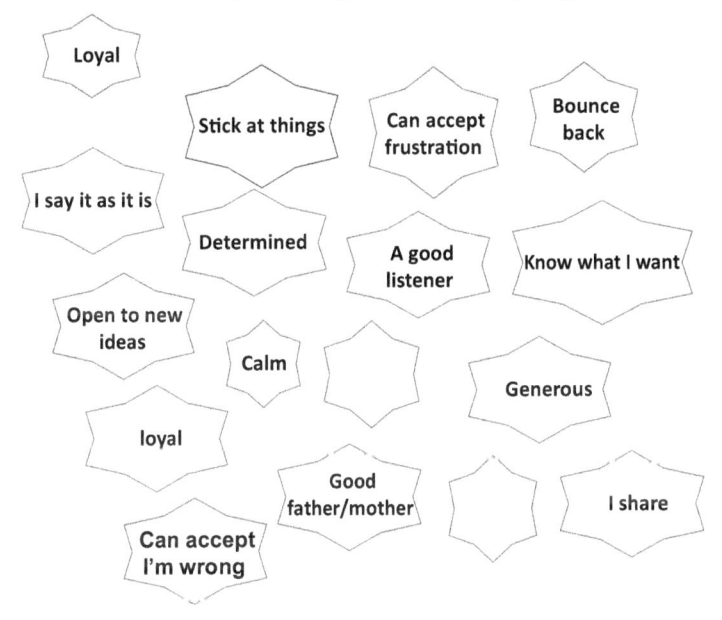

- Loyal
- Stick at things
- Can accept frustration
- Bounce back
- I say it as it is
- Determined
- A good listener
- Know what I want
- Open to new ideas
- Calm
- Generous
- loyal
- Good father/mother
- I share
- Can accept I'm wrong

How can some of my strengths help me stay non-violent and safer?

Can I see any dangers on the horizon?

What is the type of situation where I am concerned that I may possibly use violence again?

What might happen?
When?
Where?
What might I be thinking and feeling?

PNV Resource 32 Moving forward with non-violence

The key new actions, ways of thinking and dealing with my feelings that will help me be non-violent are:

Actions:

Thinking: Dealing with feelings:

My confidence about staying non-violent and safe is
0%   **100%**

Not confident at all   Totally confident

What is appropriate for me to do in relation to those who have been on the receiving end of my violence?

How will my commitment to trying to stay safe also help?

PNV Resource 33 How did I find the conversations?

```
0          1          2          3          4          5
Unhelpful                                    Extremely helpful
```

Any ideas that might make the conversations more helpful?

How was I generally feeling during much of the sessions?

- respected
- nervous
- bored
- upset
- challenged
- guilty
- uncomfortable
- interested
- learning
- angry
- relaxed
- anxious
- confused
- at ease
- changing
- put down
- shame
- not understanding

Any other circles?

How much time did I spend thinking about this work between sessions?

Do I intend to keep working at it?

Thank you for taking the time to let me know what you thought!

Appendix 2

Guidance on engaging with victims/survivors

Common violence is a complex phenomenon. As there are many factors which need to be considered before engaging with the person who uses this violence, similarly there are various factors which are relevant for the person who has been on the receiving end of the violence

Ideally, any intervention with someone who is perpetrating violence should be part of a risk assessment and decision-making process referred to in Chapter 4. This should also contain a commitment to consider and, if appropriate, prioritise the needs of the victim(s) and survivor(s). How this is done will depend on the particular circumstances of the case, and a set structure to the engagement with the victim has deliberately not been offered.

For example, in working with a young person in care who is trying to move away from gang-related violence it may not be feasible or safe to try to make contact with anyone who has been subject to the young person's violence.

On the other hand, if working with a father who wishes to have contact with a child against whom he has used previous violence, or with a carer who is continuing to live with an elderly relative, it will be important to have some sort of engagement with those who have been on the receiving end of the violence.

This should involve the provision of information about or helping the person to access groups and resources with experience in relation to the specific area of violence; for example, women's aid, nexus, community safety, victim support, etc. These groups may be able to offer more therapeutic support and give the person further information on risk and safety issues.

Information in relation to the conversations may also be shared with the victim/survivor. This does not need to be detailed. The key points are that the person has acknowledged the use of violence against the victim/survivor, is taking responsibility for this and is trying to work to get safer. The work is educational in nature, change is difficult and there are no guarantees with it. Again, with the informed consent of both parties and within the agreed plan for managing risk, the option for more communication or mediation between both parties may be considered. The conversations may be part of a restorative process that has already been embarked on between two parties or it may be the beginning of such a process.

With regard to the risk of future violence, guidance on this may be available to the victim/survivor from your agency, or from specialist, voluntary or community services involved in the relevant area of violence. If this has not been possible to access, then the safety guidance on the next page may assist in helping the victim/survivor gauge the levels of risk that they potentially face.

The person should be advised that it is not possible to predict future violence with certainty. As stated in Part I, past behaviour is often a strong indicator of future behaviour. Some of the factors in the box may be sufficient on their own to signify danger. A culmination of several or more of the factors may also signify danger. The person who has been on the receiving end of violence should be made aware of these factors to help them when considering their choices for the future.

The victim or survivor's own perspective is also important. Time and support should be given to help them think through these issues, particularly if there is to be some sort of contact or relationship with someone who has already been violent towards them.

References

Dutton, D. (1998) *The Abusive Personality: Violence and Control in Intimate Relationships*. London: The Guilford Press.

Natarajan, M. (2007) *Domestic Violence: The Five Big Questions*. Hampshire: Ashgate Publishing.

World Health Organisation (2014) *Global Statistics Report on Violence Prevention*. Geneva: WHO.

Considering your risk of experiencing future violence from a person

The following factors have all been associated with future serious violence. How many of them apply to the person who has used violence against you?
- A criminal record related to violence?
- Infliction of serious physical injuries?
- Attempts to strangle/choke?
- Use of sexually abusive behaviour?
- Violence becoming much worse or happening more often?
- Access to firearms of weapons and have these ever been used?
- Making serious threats?
- Presence of alcohol and drug-related problems or mental health difficulties such as depression, including suicide attempts or financial difficulties?
- Serious ongoing conflict or breakdown in relationship with the person?
- Controlling and/or jealousy-inspired behaviour?
- You felt driven to self-harming and suicidal thoughts as a result of the other person's actions?

Fear is a gift! You should listen to your own gut feelings and your insights.

How safe do you feel, from

0........1........2..........3........4........5.......6.......7.......8........9........10
Totally safe   **In real danger**

Why have you placed yourself at that point?

What are **your real fears and concerns** for your own safety?

Index

Note: page numbers in italic type refer to Figures; those with the page number followed by 'n' and another number refer to Notes.

aggressive responses to conflict 113–114
'Amir' (example) 12–13, 49–52, 67, 70
Angelou, Maya 44
anger 105–107, 143; anger management programmes 106; *see also* emotions
Anglo-Irish Treaty, 1921 6n2
Archibald, Christine 41n1
awareness 121–122, 150; **gift of awareness** 99; *see also* self-awareness

Banks, S. 35
biological issues in violence 26–27
Bradley, Denis 93n1
Braithwaite, J. 36
Brison, S. 24

change: cycle of change model 68–69, 130–131
character contests 39–40, 114–115, 147
check-ins (eight conversations) 58, 58–59, 60
checking out (eight conversations) 59
child abuse 3, 23, 82; children with disabilities 27–29
child brides 30n1
child development, impact of violence on 91–92, 139–140
child poverty 26
child-to-parent violence 3, 24
children: with disabilities 27–29; impact of violence on development 91–92, 139–140; physical chastisement of 22, 23, 48–49; sexual abuse by 36; sexual abuse of 17–18, 33, 46; sexual exploitation of 23, 30n1; violence against 24, 75

choice 35; power of 121–122, 150; and violence 27–28, 29
closure (eight conversations) 59, 60
coaching-inspired approaches 38
cognitive behavioural approaches 37
Commission for Victims and Survivors, Northern Ireland 87n1
common violence 3, 5, 72; addressing 28–29; and social work practice 126–127; understanding nature of 74–75, 132; *see also* violence
community-based restorative practices 4, 124
confidentiality, and the PNV process 67
conflict: 'character contests' and 'loss of face' in 39–40, 114–115; conflict resolution 115–116; non-violent responses in 115–116, 148–149; and power 116–118, 149; responses to 113–114, 146, 147–148
Conflict, power and non-violence (Conversation 7) 111, *112*, 150; content and objectives 112–118
core elements (eight conversations) 60
court reports 17
Criminal Law Act (Northern Ireland) 1967 71n4
cycle of change model 68–69, 130–131
cycle of violence 138–139

Dealing with feeling and non-violence (Conversation 6) 103, *104*, 150; content and objectives 104–118
death threats, to social workers 52
Derry shootings, 1971 94
diversity 83–84

domestic violence 28–29, 79; cessation of 47; 'gender symmetry' debate 25; and organisations' abuse of power 16–17; practitioners who are survivors of 13; social work agencies' support for victims and survivors 18; *see also* intimate partner violence

educational approaches 38
effectiveness, and the PNV process 67
eight conversations 6; overview 57–61, *58*; *see also* individual conversations
elder abuse 3, 24
'emergency relaxation' tool 109, 145–146
'emotional intelligence' 109, 145
emotions 142–143, 144; management of 108–109; and non-violence 103, *104*, 104–118; owning of 105; relationship with thinking 76–78, 108–109, 134; and violence 107–108; *see also* anger

face, loss of 114–115, 147
family-based initiatives 28
fathers: abusive 39; role in helping children to avoid violence 28; *see also* men
feelings 142–143, 144; management of 108–109; and non-violence 103, *104*, 104–118; owning of 105; relationship with thinking 76–78, 108–109, 134; and violence 107–108; *see also* anger
Feeney, Brian 41n2
Francis, Pope 28
Frankl, Victor 121–122
freeze, flight or fight response 113

Gadd, Breige 19n4
gender 79; 'gender symmetry' debate 25; and the PNV process 82–83; stereotyping 35; *see also* men; women
genes, and violence 27
Gerhardt, S. 27
gift of awareness 99
Gilligan, J. 3, 40
goals 69–70, 86, 131–132
Good Friday (Belfast) Agreement, 1998 7n2, 87n1, 111, 119, 126
Gwynne, Bailey 40

Hammer, M. 60
Harm I have caused, the (Conversation 4) 88, *89*, 150; content and objectives 89–93

hate offences 101
Havel, Vaclav 125n2
Heaney, Seamus 19n3
homosexual behaviour, legal status of in Northern Ireland 17, 19n7
House of Commons, UK, misogynistic culture of 30n4
human rights 7, 34, 36
Human Trafficking and Exploitation (Criminal Justice and Support for Victims) Act (Northern Ireland) 2015 20n8
Hume, John 5, 111, 126

'I' statements 116
inequality, and power 27–28
informed consent 57, 65–67
intellectual difficulties, and violence 27
intimate partner violence 3, 24, 25, 74, 75; *see also* domestic violence

'James' (example) 17, 47, 52
'Jane' (example) 12, 49–50, 51

Keep on keeping on towards non-violence (Conversation 8) 119, *120*; content and objectives 120–125

labelling 36
language, power of 35–36
learning, review of 121, 149–150
life balance 69–70, 86, 131–132
listening, in conflict resolution 115–116
loss of face 114–115, 147
Luckenbill, D. F. 40

Mandela, Nelson 3, 4, 19, 127
'Mary' (example) 16
Maslow, A. 70
McAleece, Mary 94
McWilliams, Monica 79
mediation 124, 153–154
men: domestic violence against 24, 25; domestic violence by 28–29, 74, 75; emotions and violence 107; gender issues in the PNV process 82–83; gender stereotyping 35; violence by 24, 25, 74, 75, 83, 101, 107, 135–136; violence by young men 24, 75
mental health problems, and violence 26
Milner, J. 36
modern-day slaves 17

motivation: motivational interviewing 37, 59; and the PNV process 67–68
Muldoon, Maura 19n5
Munroe Review of Child Protection, The: Final Report; A child-centred System 38
Musson, P. 40
My story and violence (Conversation 3) 79, *80*, 150; content and objectives 80–87
Myers, S. 36

'Nadia' (example) 48–49, 52
'Nationalist/Republican' community, Northern Ireland 7n2, 13–14
Northern Ireland: child poverty 26; continuous professional development in social work 18; serious case reviews 127
Northern Ireland Peace Process 5, 6, 58, 94, 119, 126
Northern Ireland Probation Service 33–34, 41
Northern Ireland Troubles 3, 5, 72, 79, 111; community and society violence 13–15; lack of recognition of harm caused 88

Obama, Barack 6n1
organisational culture in social work 127
organisations, abuse of power in 16–17
outcomes (eight conversations) 59

parenting-based initiatives 28
participation, and the PNV process 66–67
passive responses to conflict 113, 114
patriarchy 26, 28, 29
'peace' walls and barriers, Northern Ireland 5, 7n3, 13
'Peter' (example) 46, 47–48, 52
physical chastisement of children 22, 23
pink gloves example 39–40
Pinker, S. 37, 122
PIRA (Provisional Irish Republican Army) 14, 17
PNV (promoting non-violence) 57–59
positive psychology 37–38
positive 'triangle' of behaviour 123–124
power 116–118; and the PNV process 84–85, 136; positive aspects of 121–122, 150; and violence 27–28, 29, 136, 149
prostate cancer analogy 45–46, 49

psychological issues in violence 26
Punching holes in my thinking towards non-violence (Conversation 5) 94, *95*, 141, 150; content and objectives 95–102
punishment attacks 14, 15, 119

Rakil, M. 25
re-integrative shaming 36–37
Reid, Fr Alec 94, 119
Republic of Ireland 7n2
residential child care: social work agencies' support in 18; violence against social workers in 16
resilience perspectives 37–38
respect, and the PNV process 65–66
responsibility 29; for harm caused 92–93, 140; and violence 27–28
restorative practices 4, 124
risk, and violence 44–46, 48–52, 93, 154–155; high risk category 46; low risk category 47; medium risk category 46–47; and the PNV process 85–86; risk assessment 47–48; risk aversion 50; and 'specialist' interventions 127; working with victims and survivors 153
robberies, and female violence 24

safety, and the PNV process 66
'Sarah' (example) 21–22, 23, 24, 27, 47, 48, 49, 52
Scully-Hickey, Mathew 45
self-awareness: and personal experiences of violence 18–19; *see also* awareness
self-determination 35
self-esteem 122
sexual abusers 17–18, 36, 46
sexual exploitation of children and young people 23, 30n1
sexual harassment of women 24
sexual violence 3
'Simon' (example) 21–23, 24, 25, 26, 27, 28, 46–47, 48, 66; and the social work process 3–34, 35–37, 38, 41
Sinn Féin 14, 15
'smiling assassins' 15, 103
social justice 34–36
social work: challenges of practice 38–39; and common violence 126–127; continuous professional development in 18; definition of 7n5, 41; ethical principles 35; organisational culture 127; supervision in 127; values and

knowledge 6, 34–36, 36–38; and violence 33–41
social workers: death threats to 52; as victims of violence 5, 16
sociological issues in violence 26
'specialist' interventions 126–127
Stanko, E. A. 25
Stark, Ruth (President, International Federation of Social Workers) 33
stereotyping 34–35
strengths based perspectives 37–38
substance misuse, and violence 26
supervision, in social work 127
survivors of violence *see* victims and survivors of violence
Sustainable Development Goals 28

thinking: and emotions 76–78, 108–109, 134; negative 96, 97, 98–99; positive 99–100; safer 142; and violence 141
thinking about thinking 96–97
'thinking outside the box' exercise 99, 101–102
'Thomas' (example) 14
Thompson, Judith 19n6, 87n2
trafficking, victims of 17, 20n8
trauma: and anger 106; and the PNV process 72, 83–87; therapeutic response 4; *see also* My story and violence (Conversation 3); victims and survivors of violence
Trevithick, P. 36
Trimble, David 111
two chairs metaphor 64–65, 68

UK National Occupational Standards 41
'Unionist/Loyalist' community, Northern Ireland 7n2
United Nations: Sustainable Development Goals 28
unpredictability of violence 44–46

verbal abuse 40
victims and survivors of violence 4–5; experiences of 90, 135; guidance on engaging with 153–155; lack of recognition in Northern Ireland 88; social work agencies' support for 18
Victims Commissioner 79, 87n2
violence: and author's social work career 2–3; biological issues 26–27; choice, responsibility and power in 27–28, 29; in communities and society 13–15; cycle of 138–139; definition of 22–23; effects of 137–138; and emotions 107–108; explanations for 25–28; in families of origin and relationships 11–13; literature and research on 5, 21–30; measurement of 23–25; personal encounters with 11–19; in professional and working lives 16–18; psychological issues 26; and risk 44–52; and social work 33–41; sociological issues 26; and thoughts and feelings 76–78; unpredictability of 44–46; *see also* common violence

What is there to talk about? (Conversation 2) 72, *73*, 149; content and objectives 73–78
'Why' question (Conversation 1) 62, *63*, 149; content and objectives 63–71
women: gender issues in the PNV process 83; gender stereotyping 35; violence against 24, 29, 75; violence by 24–25, 75, 83–84
World Health Organisation 23

young men, violence by 3, 24, 75
young people: brain development 109; sexual exploitation 23, 30n1